Co-Create

Co-Create

Harnessing the Human Element in Project Management

Steve Martin

BEP BUSINESS EXPERT PRESS

Co-Create: Harnessing the Human Element in Project Management

Copyright © Business Expert Press, LLC, 2017.

First published in 2017 by
Business Expert Press, LLC
222 East 46th Street, New York, NY 10017
www.businessexpertpress.com

ISBN-13: 978-1-63157-627-0 (paperback)
ISBN-13: 978-1-63157-628-7 (e-book)

Business Expert Press Portfolio and Project Management Collection

Collection ISSN: 2156-8189 (print)
Collection ISSN: 2156-8200 (electronic)

Cover and interior design by Exeter Premedia Services Private Ltd., Chennai, India

First edition: 2017

10 9 8 7 6 5 4 3 2 1

Printed in the United States of America.

To Mary

Abstract

Successfully moving an organization forward is a complex task. Historically professional organizations, like the Project Management Institute, have done a fine job of providing best practices and technical tools to support Project Managers in the field. These tools will continue to be critical in the future. The opportunity now is to add to that body of knowledge by addressing, more completely, the human experience. In reviewing the literature, practitioners and academics alike have noted that committed teams play an important role in creating exceptional project outcomes. What has been missing is the connection between what's known about employee engagement and commitment, from a general management perspective, and a practical method to integrate that knowledge with project management tools.

This book will provide a comprehensive map for project managers to learn about the human experience during a project. It will present specific practices for generating commitment that can be easily incorporated by project managers. The Co-Create Model presents a conceptual understanding and a method not currently found in the literature.

Keywords

commitment, creating team commitment, engaged teams, high performing teams, project management, project teams

Contents

Acknowledgments

I must begin my thanks by acknowledging the best decision I've ever made—asking Mary to be my wife. Mary has been my primary source of support and inspiration over the last 33 years in addition to being my best friend. Her love has sustained me through many ups and downs and provided the foundation for my personal and professional growth.

Thank you to our son Joe and the grandchildren, Julia and Joseph, who have taught me that life has its challenges and that all can be overcome with love—especially if good food and Graeters Ice Cream is involved.

I would like to thank my parents, Rose and Tom, who set the foundation for all that I am. My mother taught me about empathy and the importance of faith. My father taught me the importance of humor, responsibility, and how to work.

Looking back, I am amazed by how the many wonderful and talented people have shown up in my life at just the right time. To that end, I would like to thank:

Jack Roberts—who, at the age of 15, taught me to fly, to see the world differently, and appreciate the unseen forces that must be balanced to fly successfully. Little did I realize at the time how important this understanding would be to the rest of my personal and business life.

Roy Nelson—who was a model of a way of life connecting business with family and quietly making a positive difference in the world. He was very much a second father figure.

At Northern Kentucky University I signed up for an undergraduate class in Organizational Psychology with George Manning. Like most college freshmen, I didn't really have a clear idea of what I wanted to do with my life. That first class sparked something inside—I was intrigued with psychology and its application to work. George was my first professional mentor who took me on consulting assignments and provided a model for how education and psychology could be applied to help organizations become not only more effective but also better places to be. George's positive energy and willingness to spend time with me was invaluable.

Graduate school at the University of Cincinnati was all about Bill Stewart. Bill ran our program in the School of Education and was famous for his stories. He was a character with a diverse set of life experiences—career veteran, entrepreneur, and educator. He continually amazed us with his ability to repurpose stories to fit the idea he was illustrating. I appreciated his creativity and positive outlook on life.

My local organization development (OD) network has also provided help, Peter Block who transformed my thinking about engagement and accountability, Steve McMillian, Jean Lapoint, Barry Morris, Lisa Haneburg, and Mike Webb all have helped in one way or another in advancing my thinking.

From Xavier University, John Van Kirk and Phil Jones were both major contributors. Phil taught me about process improvement methodologies. John developed my strategic thinking ability and how to buy a good bottle of red wine for less than $10. I've often marveled at how abstract concepts become so much clearer after a second glass!

I'd like to acknowledge all the good people I've worked with at Hubert. For the last 26 years they educated and walked with me as we explored the best way to make things better. The walk was far from a straight line. As we made the journey, there were more than a few dead ends and what I really appreciate is that we learned from them and started out again. I'm sure there were times when they wondered if I had lost my mind but that was never said—it was always about what we were going to try next. Throughout the book you will also see their fine work in the form of the examples I've used. I'd especially like to recognize Patti Chesney, Greg Hubert, Tina Beccaccio, and Tom Marine.

Specifically, Bart Kohler is the best boss a person can have. His authenticity, empathy, humanistic values, and business acumen are unparalleled and a significant driver for Hubert's success. He has supported my work and challenged me continuously ("Martin I like it but can you do it faster"). He is both my boss and friend.

At the executive level—Greg Ollinger, John Ebbert, Carlin Stamm, Mark Green, Mark Rudy, Mark Woodrow, Jeff Shelton, Tim Lansing Dick Thoene, Andy Hallock, all have been beyond generous in teaching me about their disciplines and how businesses really work. I could not have received a better business education at Harvard.

Lisa Van Sant and Laura Hawley have provided my ongoing education in Human Resources. They are HR experts and get-it-done people who have freed me up to wander off to explore new OD roads.

I owe a major debt to my co-traveler on this journey, Robb MacFarlane. Robb and I have worked together for over 20 years in the OD department. I greatly appreciate Robb's patience and ability to work my broad ideas down from 50,000 feet to how to use an idea to get something done. He is unique in his ability to span the conceptual to the concrete. He is very smart and has a great sense of humor. I could not have had a better colleague.

I also want to call out the uncountable number of project teams over the years. The Co-Create model would not have emerged without the testing, changing, and retesting that occurred as we applied it to real issues and opportunities facing Hubert.

Throughout this project I've distinctly felt divine guidance. My hope is that sharing this model will help make the world just a little bit better. And if it does, my mission is complete.

Introduction

There's a moment during every successful project when things come together, the team gels, and energy soars. It feels magical. The day-to-day work comes together to generate commitment, clarity, and momentum. Something new, surprising, and useful is created. It's a beautiful thing!

If your organization is like mine, a lot of work gets done through teams and projects. Over the last 26 years, my colleagues and I at the Hubert Company have been honing and using a process we call the *Co-Create model*. This book describes the model and tells our story. We use the Co-Create model for all our large projects. Our employees participate in this work to improve the business—they are deeply engaged and committed to create a better future. The model establishes a framework from which team excellence can flourish.

Why Co-Create?

This model has been shown to provide:

- Excellent project execution—Co-Create is an integrated process that helps team members to (1) create focus on the project's purpose and goals, (2) manage tasks, (3) build commitment, and (4) collaborative relationships.
- Change leadership—Co-Create uses proven change management and engagement principles (see Addendum C) to enable team members to cope with the fast pace of change and build agility into their work. The model provides project leaders a roadmap to help guide the team.
- Employee commitment—My belief is that commitment is the secret to high performance. When teams are highly committed they will do whatever is required to achieve success. It's more important than project management tools or even having the optimal skill-set around the table. The

question is can a project manager develop commitment
intentionally? The answer to this is yes! High levels of
commitment naturally grow out of the experience.

And finally we have no choice but to co-create. We are forever connecting and creating with others. Organizations exist to do what no individual can. So the choice is whether or not we co-create *intentionally*. The
Co-Create model provides a path to help teams develop solutions that
create value for all.

You will likely recognize some of the processes and tools included in
the Co-Create model. We have pulled these tools from the recognized
thought leaders to create the model. The combination and integration of
these methods, with a <u>key addition</u>, is what makes this model unique and
the results extraordinary.

Commitment Is Key to the Co-Create Model

Traditional project and change management techniques have taken the
profession a long way. The current opportunity is to maximize the human
element. We need to understand that the human journey as a project
progresses and how to increase team member commitment. One of the
key outcomes of using this model is the high level of employee commitment generated.

Comprehensive

Co-Create also integrates our individual and organizational goals and
objectives as they play out in a team environment. It brings to the fore
the idea that we are all working for something greater than ourselves.
Each contribution makes a difference—it changes the world one thought
and action at a time.

Who This Book Is for

I have written this book primarily for practitioners—project managers—team leaders and members—and organization development pro-
fessionals who train and develop teams. I have also included important

considerations and beneficial information for leaders who want to improve performance and engagement.

What's Next?

In the coming pages I will review the Co-Create model. It contains four underlying big ideas used to generate engagement. The core of the model illustrates the project journey—it specifically depicts the task, team, and individual phases of project work and change.

The Co-Create model offers a way of working that creates high levels of commitment and excellent project outcomes. Our team members like using the model because it enables them to do their best work, experience meaning and purpose, participate, collaborate, and create a better organization. They make a difference.

Crafting and using the Co-Create model has changed my life and filled my work with purpose. I hope you and your teams apply the model and enjoy the same benefits of its use.

> *"Never doubt that a small group of thoughtful, committed citizens can change the world. Indeed, it is the only thing that ever has."*
> —Margaret Mead

CHAPTER 1

The Co-Create Model—
A Map for the Journey

When we were developing the Co-Create model, we asked ourselves how we could combine what we felt was most important (the ideas) with best practices from project management, change management, and team development. We continued to tweak the model until we felt we had an excellent practice. This chapter describes the four underlying ideas and then uses six distinct phases to help teams achieve results.

Figure 1.1 offers a visual description of the Co-Create model. At first, it might look a bit complicated, but it is actually very straightforward. There are six phases that teams use to launch and complete projects and

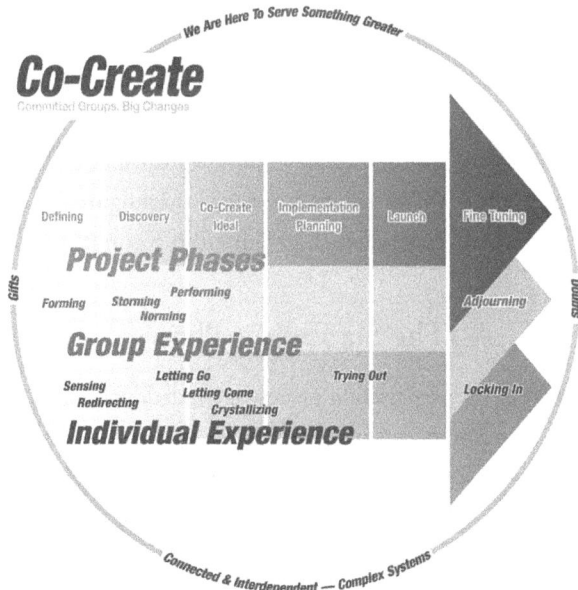

Figure 1.1 The Co-Create model

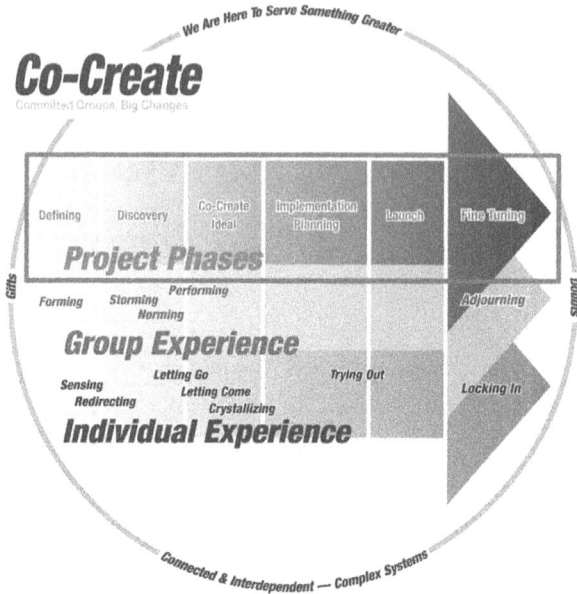

Figure 1.2 Highlighting the "project" phases

produce results. These six phases are highlighted in Figure 1.2 and include defining, discovery, co-create the ideal, implementation planning, execution, and fine tuning.

The project phases help us build robust solutions to new opportunities. These six phases keep us on track and remind us to spend time where it will be most beneficial.

People complete projects, so during the work we attend to two types of experiences, the team or group experience (highlighted in Figure 1.3) and each individual's experience (highlighted in Figure 1.4).

The Six Project Phases

The six project phases represent a process for individual engagement, team creation, and project execution. Each phase of the Co-Create model is explained in more detail in the coming chapters, but here is a brief description:

1. **Defining**: We spend a lot of time at the beginning of each project to ensure that we adequately define and describe what we want the

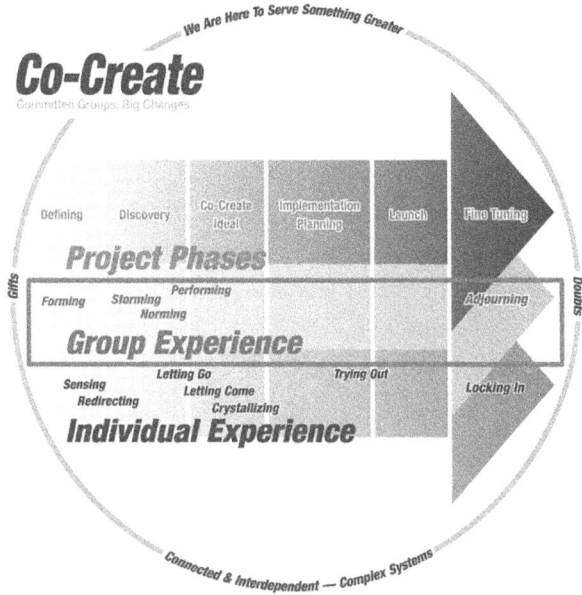

Figure 1.3 Highlighting the "group" experience

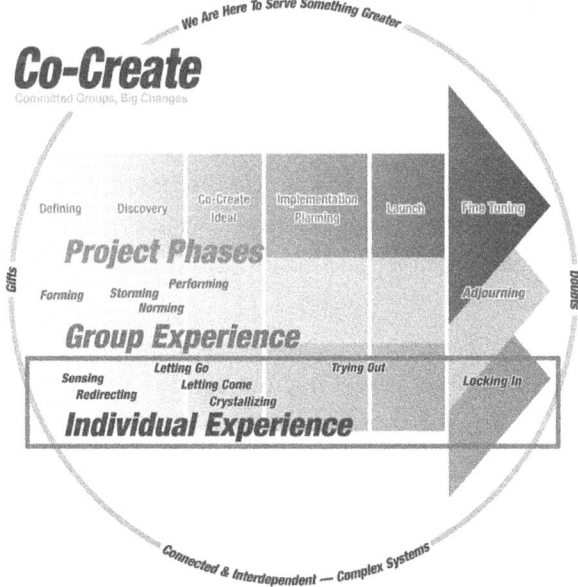

Figure 1.4 Highlighting the "individual" experience

project to accomplish and the roles people will play in helping to support and manifest project goals. During this critical first phase, every project owner creates a white paper (or Charter) for their project. We have found that the time invested upfront improves everything that happens throughout the project.

2. **Discovery**: During the discovery phase, the team creates a robust and detailed picture of the current state. All team members participate and this tends to be a very energizing process. The information they generate is critical to analyzing and creating solutions that work.

3. **Co-create the ideal**: The team leader guides the group in generating possibilities and creating a plan forward based on the whitepaper from Phase 1 and the current state analysis from Phase 2. They discuss, agree upon, and document the conditions for success for the project.

4. **Implementation planning**: During Phase 4, the team gets into the nitty-gritty to determine what needs to happen, by when, and by whom. This phase is the most similar to traditional project planning processes. As you will discover in Chapter 6, however, our action plans are much more than a long list of to-dos. They contain methods to enhance successful implementation.

5. **Launch**: The team launches the project and because their conversations have been open and collaborative thus far they are able to flexibly implement the project plan and meet or beat the desired results.

6. **Fine tuning**: As the name implies, this phase of the project enables the team to make additional adjustments (they measure and adjust throughout the project) and tie up any loose ends. The team closes out the project.

These project phases ensure that our projects are well planned and executed. Most organizations focus on Phase 4 and Phase 5, but few start and end with the deliberate and open project management practices like we use in the Co-Create model. The extra work we do upfront serves several important purposes and improves our results. Do our projects take longer? I would argue no. We start slower and with more initial discussions, but this work paves the way for a less troublesome project implementation with fewer post-implementation issues.

At the same time the team is working through the six project phases, they are experiencing their work as a team and as individuals. How people work together and experience change is important. Until we developed the Co-Create model we did not have a way to proactively help our team members understand what they were going to go through. We also didn't have a comprehensive map for our project leaders. Taking the mystery out has benefited both.

You can probably recall a situation where a well-planned project underperformed because of poor team dynamics or low collaboration. And you may know individuals who are more talented than is evident by their contribution to the team. The group experience and individual experience elements of the model build in the structure we need to ensure that we consider the people part of the project.

The Group Experience

To build a great team experience, we use the Tuckman model of team development (Tuckman 1977). Teams go through recognizable stages of development—and they go into and out of these stages many times during their work together. Dr. Bruce Tuckman presented a model that identified five stages that teams experience. Figure 1.5 shows the stages of the Tuckman model, which are: Forming, Storming, Norming, Performing, and Adjourning. Tuckman's model explains that as the team develops maturity and ability, relationships and coping skills strengthen. Project setbacks or victories will also affect how the team works together. For the Co-Create Model, we have overlaid the stages of team development with

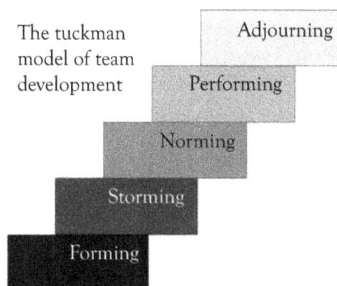

The tuckman model of team development

Adjourning

Performing

Norming

Storming

Forming

Figure 1.5 Tuckman model of team development

our six project phases. We do some very specific activities throughout the project's life cycle to help our teams work well together and quickly identify and deal with any setbacks.

I am frequently asked whether the need to do team development is reduced as team members work on more than one project together. The answer is yes and no. We certainly benefit from the synergies, relationship building, and learning that have occurred on previous projects. That said, every team is a new team and project roles and tasks are different. Sources of potential conflict or discomfort are often tied to particular topics or tasks, and so we need to attend to the team's developmental stages—in some degree—on every project. By understanding the stages of team development and the corresponding team leadership and executive support actions that best support each stage (and movement to the next), we have found that we can better help teams do their best work. Here is a brief description of the stages of the Tuckman model of team development:

1. **Forming**: The initial stage of team development where members are getting oriented to one another and seeking to understand their roles and boundaries.
2. **Storming**: This stage of team development is characterized by style clashes, conflict, and working out differences. We find that familiar team members can go back to this phase when a new project or task brings disagreements to the surface.
3. **Norming**: The team is getting to know each other and is working through how to work well together. Their efforts look and feel more cohesive.
4. **Performing**: The team is utilizing the strengths of their relationships to get more done. Their ability to collaborate and solve problems is a competitive edge. Roles are flexible but clear.
5. **Adjourning**: The team creates closure for their work and feels complete in the task of marking the project's end.

Teams can skip forward or backward in development when new members join or when they are affected by unsettling changes. In addition to group health and drama, we also need to deal with how each team member is experiencing the demands of the project, interactions with his or her colleagues, and the work processes.

The Individual Experience

To help our employees connect with their individual experience we draw upon the work of Peter Senge, Otto Sharmer, and Betty Sue Flowers. In their 2005 book called *Presence: Exploring Profound Change In People, Organizations, and Society* (Senge et al. 2005), the authors offered a model of individual change or transition called the U model that we use throughout the six project phases of the Co-Create model. Here is a quick review of the elements of the U model:

1. **Sensing (suspending)**: Gathering and considering information and mental models about the current state.
2. **Redirecting**: Seeing things from a systemic and holistic way. Becoming aware that we may need to think about things differently and modify their current work activities.
3. **Letting go**: Letting go of definitions of success and mental models that no longer serve our goals. Opening up our minds to new possibilities. Being more coachable.
4. **Letting come**: This is the creative work that comes as much from the heart as the head. The essence or seed of the solution becomes conscious.
5. **Crystallizing**: Bringing together the new ideas to build a path forward.
6. **Trying out (prototyping)**: Experimenting with new approaches. Learning from the process of trying. This step involves iterations—making adjustments based on the learning derived from trying it out.
7. **Locking in (institutionalizing)**: Adopting and forming new habits and regimens. The new becomes your natural way.

The U model helps us understand and improve individual growth and development. By discussing this model at the beginning of a project it helps each individual team member know what's coming. As the project progresses it provides a touch point for additional discussion especially when points of view diverge or the group is having difficulty with an idea that may be very different than current thinking. The Co-Create model would be incomplete without the individual experience phases.

The practices we use as part of the Co-Create model reinforce the importance of paying attention to the project, the group dynamics, and individual's reactions to the work. Ignoring or skipping any will reduce results. The task of the team leader is to be conscience of the interactions of the project, team, and individual phases, and to manage the project and these three perspectives simultaneously. This is where the art and science of facilitation and team performance converge.

Roles and Responsibilities

Many people, united by a purpose, help ensure team performance and success. Each project is different, but we typically define the following roles. These folks ensure that each project is well defined, aligned with the strategic plan, and executed well.

- Executive group—This is typically the president and the vice presidents who are responsible for identifying the major issues or strategic opportunities facing the organization. Their job is to provide high-level direction about what needs to be developed to support the strategy.
- Sponsor—The sponsor is a vice president or senior manager who translates the strategic direction into a project. When projects span functional areas, either the two VPs co-sponsor the project or the president will serve as the sponsor. The sponsor contracts with the team facilitator for project design. The sponsor secures the required resources—people, money, time, and so on—and works with the project owner to write the project whitepaper. Once the work begins, the sponsor and project owner monitor the project to ensure alignment and are available to help with critical decisions as appropriate.

- Project owner—Most often this is a director level manager who has responsibility for the functional area where the majority of the project is taking place. They write the white-paper with some help, attend all team meetings and actively participate in the work as a team member. This person is the primary contact for, and coworker of, the team facilitator. They work closely together to manage the approach, specific meeting agendas, and the many details of the project. The day-to-day leadership is shared by the project owner and the team facilitator.
- Team facilitator—This person is responsible to facilitate the team's process. For major projects this role is fulfilled by someone from a corporate organizational development or HR function or an outside consultant. For smaller projects, the team facilitator is someone from a functional area who has been trained in the Co-Create system. This includes leading team meetings, developing meeting notes, and working with team members as they develop the discovery (Phase 2) visuals and design implementation communication or training programs.
- Team members—The team is comprised of front line employees who represent key stakeholder groups and bring specific expertise to the work. Their job is to provide information and input and to participate in the implementation process.
- End users—The people outside the team who will be receiving or using the project output, which could be a new workflow process, software changes, or a new structure. The team may consider input from this group during the project. The team keeps this group updated on the progress of the project.
- Outside vendors—External partners who provide products or services to the group. Examples include software vendors and legal advice.

These roles, and any others as applicable, are specifically identified in the project whitepaper, which is completed during Phase 1 of the project.

Frequently Asked Questions

Before I explore each phase of the Co-Create model in detail, here are the answers to the questions I most get from people when they first learn about our approach.

Q: How long are the projects and how large are the project teams?

A: Major waterfall projects have ranged from three months to two years in length. The average project is 9 to 12 months long. The team size typically ranges from 6 to 10 members.

Q: This model uses a waterfall approach for projects. Can it be used with Agile methods.

A: Absolutely! At a high level Agile compresses the time and scope of projects allowing faster implementation of project components. You can insert the Agile method of your choosing into the project phase area of the model. At the end of the day you still have the opportunity to enhance commitment beginning with the big ideas at the beginning of the sprint. Additionally the team and individual dynamics do not change—unless artificial intelligence eventually replaces us all!

Q: How long did it take for you to get buy-in from senior leader on the more "touchy-feely" aspects of the model?

A: The soft side of the model must be consistent with the organizations culture. If the culture is conducive and the model is properly explained, the business case for the soft side is readily apparent and hard to argue. The model was ultimately embraced because of the results we achieved.

Q: Does using the model pay off financially?

A: Yes it does. Two projects that I worked on were (1) to reduce cost of goods by $1 million and (2) acquired $10 million in business, which had to be completed in a 60-day period. It's difficult to estimate the total financial contribution of all the projects using this model over the years. If I had to venture a guess about either the total sales or profit impact I would say it influenced somewhere between $50 and $100 million.

Q: What if I am worried that my organization is not ready for something like this?

A: You will find an organization readiness checklist in the conclusion, which starts on page 66.

Q: How is participation on a team connected to your performance management system?

A: For many of our key positions project participation is listed as one of the responsibilities on their performance management document. For individuals who participate only occasionally on teams it is not formally listed as a responsibility and would be acknowledged in the comments or as an addendum to the performance management document.

Q: How does a team member balance day-to-day responsibilities with project work?

A: Our expectation is that individuals figure out how best to balance their overall workload. For example, they may be able to juggle it all success-fully and meet their obligations. They may approach coworkers and ask for help to cover some aspect of their responsibilities for a period of time. Or they may negotiate with their boss about delaying a certain task until a project is over. The bottom line is that the individual is responsible to figure out the plan—to use their creativity to see what's possible and to ask for help. I would encourage them to begin with the question "How will I meet my daily obligations *and* participate on this team?" In our culture, we have a core value around service to others—this is a perfect opportunity for a coworker to lend a hand.

Q: Do team members follow through on their project assignments? How do you ensure accountability?

A: This has not been a major issue for us. Situations do come up that require flexibility but overall the use of simple project management tech-niques works well. For instance, the facilitator captures all the action items at the end of each meeting along with the responsible party and due dates. This information is documented in the meeting minutes and is available in OneNote. The facilitator then begins the next meeting by reviewing the action items from the previous meeting. If someone is having difficulty getting an action item done we use that as an opportunity to explore the issues. In the rare case where an individual continues to miss deadlines I've seen the group exert pressure on them or if the problem is legitimate, invariably someone will volunteer to help out.

Considerations for Leaders

The leaders at Hubert have supported the organic growth and development of the Co-Create model. They have seen the tangible and cultural benefits that this way of working brings to the business. As a leader, what questions do you have about an approach like Co-Create? I recommend that you gather a small group of your peers to discuss the type of performance environment you want to create and whether this approach might get you there.

Conclusion

I hope I have piqued your interest in how the Co-Create model works. In the coming chapters, I will drill down on how we use each phase of the model and I will share several specific examples from real projects and project teams.

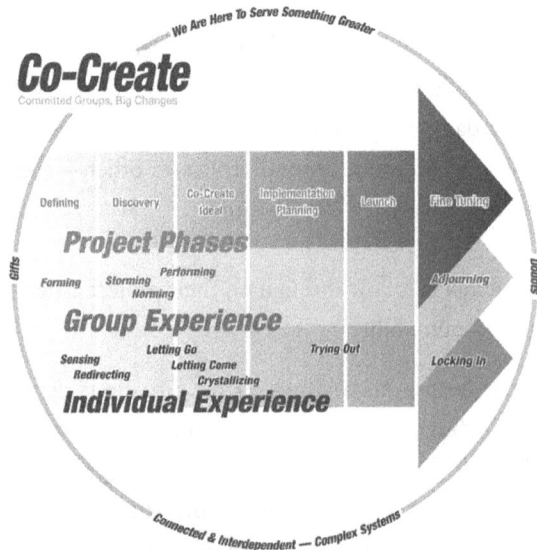

CHAPTER 2

The Big Ideas

The Co-Create model was developed to align our actions with four principles. We call these principles the "big ideas" and they connect directly to specific stages of the model and provide teams with a source of inspiration and energy to complete the work. The principles are the "soft stuff" that creates high levels of commitment and supports the manifestation of the "hard stuff." In practice these four ideas are discussed at the first team meeting. They are presented as a series of questions by the project manager/facilitator in four distinct conversations. The following information will give you a conceptual understanding of the ideas. Later in the book you'll find specific information about how to apply them. These discussions begin the commitment-building process. The work happens in the container created.

Big Idea #1: We are Here to Serve Something Greater than Ourselves

Sample Project Team Questions:

- Specifically how does this idea relate to this project?
- What is the "something greater" for this project?

Life inside any organization today is demanding. Technology has fundamentally changed how we work and the Internet has created a level of transparency shifting the competitive landscape. Faster, better, cheaper has become the ongoing mantra. Day-to-day existence often revolves around working a long to-do list, responding to countless e-mails and attending meetings. Performance is measured based on how well and how quickly we deliver results. This focused perspective, while required to crank out the work, can cause us to lose sight of the bigger picture. It can isolate us and make us think that our only purpose is to get *our* work done and survive the day. But no matter how task-driven the workplace is, there is a more compelling reason to do the work. We are part of something bigger—an unfolding story of which we play an important role.

We are here to serve something greater than ourselves by co-creating a better world. In the broadest sense it is a universal purpose. *Better* can be defined in many ways—it may look like a more effective process, product, department, or organization. Or it may look like a productive meeting between two departments where there have been past tensions or misunderstandings. Or it may be an authentic and caring conversation between two people. Whatever form it takes *better* is any improvement in the current state.

What does it look like to be operating from a mindset of creating a better world? Outside of business it inspires us to help people who are suffering, the environment, and creatures of all types. In business we are here to bring increasing value to *all* stakeholders. How can we improve the outcomes for our customers, owners, employees, suppliers, and communities? When we do this, our work makes a difference and has purpose.

But what about when things don't go so well—when we hit roadblocks or constraints? How do we deal with "problems?" Problems are a natural disruptive force or energy and essentially feed the creative process by communicating the need for change. They indicate a situation requiring our attention. Problems present an opportunity to continue the movement forward by telling us where we have work to do.

The Co-Create model uses the power of purpose by exploring project goals several layers deeper than the task level. At the first project team meeting we ask the group to explore the "why" for the project. Our teams discuss how the project is aligned with the organization's greater purpose and strategic objectives. When we do this the groups' perspective noticeably shifts—the seeds have been planted that will result in increases in commitment, focus, and energy, and amazing things happen.

The power of purpose ultimately rests with the individuals who are part of the project. I'd like to go a little deeper into individual purpose— what it is and how it creates commitment—starting with a definition.

Damon, Menon, and Bronk have created the following definition of purpose:

> "Purpose is a stable and generalized intention to accomplish something that is at once meaningful to the self and of consequence beyond the self."
>
> Damon, Menon, and Bronk (2003)

It is fundamentally a mindset—a perspective that shifts our self-awareness, behavior, and creates better outcomes.

Another take on this topic begins with the question: Is your work a job, a career, or a calling? Sociologist, Robert Bellah, provides a simple model to help people think about their work and the role it plays in their lives. You might want to think about people you work with—it's not hard to attach faces and names to each category!

> **Job** = necessary evil—I work to survive.
> **Career** = my purpose is to get to the next rung on the ladder— my satisfaction is from attaining my next career goal.
> **Calling** = my purpose is to make meaning from 9 to 5 and somehow make the world a better place.
>
> Bellah et al. (1985).

The point is that individual motivation, commitment, and results increase greatly as you move from the mindset of your work as a job, to a career, to a calling.

Making Meaning

So how can you experience this directly? What characteristics drive meaning and how does it look in practice on the job or when you're working on a team?

- Freedom to apply your thoughts and ideas—to make decisions
- An opportunity to use a number of your skills

- An understanding of how your work contributes to a tangible product or service
- A sense of how the product or service matters to the community

To sum it up we all start with a universal purpose, one that resonates across time and cultures, that we are here (on earth, in this job, in this relationship) to use our gifts to make the world we touch better.

The most effective, impactful people and organizations are clear and intentional about their purpose. It's consciously understood and acted on.

The Co-Create model provides the opportunity to explicitly bring the idea of purpose, both individually and organizationally, into the project with discussion of Big Idea #1 thus increasing commitment.

Big Idea #2: We are Connected and Interdependent— Existing in Complex Systems

Sample Project Team Questions:

- Who are the stakeholders for this project?
- What are their interests?
- What's at stake for each?
- What connections and partnerships will be needed to succeed?

This is a hard concept to grasp and apply in organizations experiencing nonstop change, particularly when employees are feeling guarded, insecure, and understaffed. When we are stressed, overwhelmed, and/or worried, we feel vulnerable making it hard to connect. Our focus can become very internal. Connections are not always evident making it difficult to see how our actions impact others. It takes time to understand and include our upstream and downstream internal customers in our work. It may also be difficult to move beyond self-interest (many of us don't even realize that this motivation is driving our work).

The truth is we do not exist in isolation and can't accomplish anything significant without others. Our thoughts lead to actions. Like a pebble thrown in the water, every action reverberates and causes ripples. What we do WILL result in intended and unintended consequences.

Sometimes we are aware of the impact of our actions and sometimes we are not. Either way, the impact occurs. That is why believing and working in alignment with this principle is so critical. To be successful, we need to become aware of connections and their consequences.

At work, this education begins with understanding how your individual job creates value to your immediate co-workers or department. It then extends to how your department contributes to other departments and the work they do. It continues outward by an understanding of how all departments come together to create value for key stakeholders.

Another benefit of aligning our actions with this idea is that it changes the nature of the conversations we have when we are working on change projects where there is serious pain. It is easy to place blame on others— feeling that if they only would do their job (in a way that's best for us!) our problems would go away. Systems thinking—awareness of complexity and connections—helps us let go of dysfunctional blame or judgment and creates a mindset of exploration or discovery.

The structures and processes within the Co-Create model ensure that team members work in ways that recognize and utilize their interconnectedness. They come to understand that each connection is vital for the whole to function optimally and that their work is part of a complex system. The best way to alter and improve outcomes is by working within the context of the whole.

Big Idea #3: Doubt

Sample Project Team Questions:

- What doubts or concerns do you have about this project?
- What's at risk for you?
- How might this impact your daily work?

Given that we are here to make the world a better place and are interconnected, it is important that we explore what might be in the way of making progress as individuals and as a team. Individually, we have the opportunity and responsibility to say "yes" or "no" to change. Engaging in the work can feel like leaning into a high wind and stepping forward. Do we do this or do we avoid it because it's too uncomfortable?

The Co-Create model helps individuals identify, explore, and move past sources of resistance and barriers to getting the work done.

Doubts or concerns are always present. We might feel fear, worry, or mistrust when faced with a project that involves a lot of changes. Individually we worry whether we will be successful and whether our skills will still be needed and valued in the new reality. We may worry that we won't be able to measure up. The Co-Create model helps team members identify their fears, discuss them openly, and build confidence about what they will be able to contribute as things change. We believe that this is a critical part of the process and every bit as important as creating a robust timeline or task list.

The model also invites teams to deal openly with their concerns. If they disagree with the assumptions that define a goal, the process offers them a safe and consistent way to bring their ideas and apprehensions forward. Since it is a regular part of working the project, teams develop the ability to be candid and comfortable to challenge ideas.

Can You Say "No?"

We always have the choice to say yes or no to what life presents to us. As Peter Block likes to say… "if you can't say no your yes has no meaning." This conscious choice is essential to making any commitment and having the energy to follow through on the work. In a business setting, the expectation is for employees to support the ongoing development of the organization. If the executive leadership team has done their work well it should be readily apparent why a project is important to maintaining or improving the organization's ability to compete. If for some reason an individual disagrees with or finds themselves working on a project that violates their values then the choice they should make is to say no to being involved. Depending on the circumstances it may be acceptable to decline or in extreme cases it may require them to find a new organization more aligned with their values and vision where they can say yes. At the end of the day we must all keep our integrity *and* be moving forward.

This underlying idea asks us all to engage and explore any doubts or concerns we have with the work. Avoiding our doubts doesn't cause them to go away—rather they will come back usually in a dysfunctional form. The Co-Create model provides space where it is both safe to be candid and where teams are expected to articulate and think through concerns. The interesting thing about this conversation is that solutions are not required—or maybe even possible. The act of discussing doubts is what's important because the result is a decrease or release of the negative energy allowing the work to proceed.

Big Idea #4: We are Here to Contribute Our Gifts

Sample Project Team Questions:

- What gifts are you bringing to this project?
- Specifically what knowledge, skills, or past experience will help the project succeed?

Every member of the team brings something unique to the project. It might be analytic skills, a visionary creative mindset, the ability to connect with large groups of people, or a *get it done* action orientation. It could also be certain technical expertise or prior experience relevant to this project. We know that for the project to be successful we have to create the environment for these skills to be used fully.

This model is designed to combine the gifts of many people in order to create something no one individual could have on their own. That is a key task for the project leader and facilitator.

We also help our employees discover and understand their unique talents. When we first started using the Co-Create model, we were surprised by how many people had trouble articulating their strengths. We now start each project with conversation about what each team member is bringing to the project. When we are conscious of our gifts, we can use them more often and other team members can tap into them.

We need to have the right group of people (with the right gifts) working on the right project. A team selection and assignment process creates an environment where diverse talents come together and create an environment of respect, collaboration, and results orientation. We need everyone's skills to remain competitive and to succeed.

Considerations for Leaders

These four big ideas advocate for a highly engaged and empowered approach to project management and team leadership. Leaders must ask themselves "does your organization embrace these beliefs?" Do these ideas fit your culture? If not, what might be possible if they did? Could you use this approach to evolve the culture? Or is the gap too large and it's time to stop reading now? The truth is the culture must be open to this approach. If you're working in a "eat our young" highly competitive culture or one where the boss must always have the right answer this approach is not appropriate.

Summary

The four underlying ideas bring the Co-Create model to life. The four conversations at the beginning of a project create a container for the work, which enable higher levels of commitment. This is perhaps the most important distinction between the Co-Create model and other methods used to implement project and change.

CHAPTER 3

Phase 1

Phase 1 is called *Defining* and requires the time be spent ensuring that the team understands the project, its goals, and roles of each team member. It is important to invest this time and build relationships. Phase 1 work sets the trajectory for the project and the team's performance.

For each phase, one through six, I will follow the format of discussing what's happening from three perspectives; the project, the team, and the individual. I will also cover some of the pitfalls to avoid and considerations for leaders.

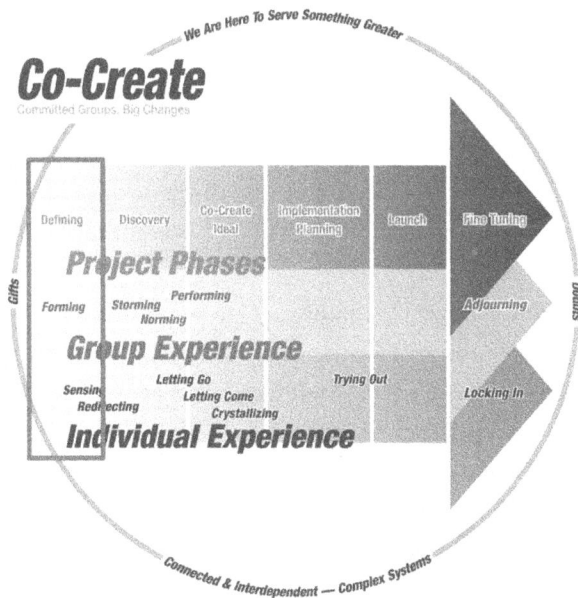

What's Happening at Phase 1?

For the Project—Defining

The goal is to ensure that the task and business case for change is clear. This requires a considerable amount of work. The project owner writes a white paper with the input of the sponsor and other stakeholders. The white paper becomes the guide and launch charter for the team.

We do not advocate the use of a particular format or template for the white paper. We will coach the project owner on the types of information they should cover and we provide them two books that offer helpful ideas:

- *The Team Handbook*, by Peter Scholtes, Brian Joiner, and Barbara Streibel.
- *Change the Way You Lead Change: Leadership Strategies that Really Work* by David Herold and Donald Fedor.

The owner, sponsor, and key stakeholders discuss each component of the whitepaper until they agree and have a clear definition of the project. This important work can take weeks or months to complete.

Co-Create project white papers combine information typically found in business plans, project plans, and executive briefings. Each is unique in its content, voice, and length, but they all cover the following sections:

- Situation summary: Definition of the opportunity including its purpose and an analysis of the situation/market, and the internal and external environment. What needs changing and why? Who will the change most impact? This section might also share new learning that is the impetus for the change. How will this change benefit the business and how does it support our strategies and mission?
- Scope, phases, and resources: Project scope, resources, and roles, including broad project timelines. Specific team members are identified.
- Deliverables: Specific project objectives including outcomes, measures of success, and anticipated impacts to the business.

For the Team—Forming

The team facilitator guides the group through a 2- to 3-hour kick-off meeting that we use to jump-start the team development process. Here is a typical agenda for this first meeting:

- Review the meeting agenda.
- Initial self-introductions.
- Review the whitepaper.
- Review the Co-Create model.
- Discuss the "Big Idea" questions (something greater; connections; gifts; doubt). Record if appropriate.
- Generate group norms and record them. This creates an intentional starting point. This really comes to life when the group works through storming in Phase 2 and truly develops an understanding of what norming looks like in practice.
- Housekeeping: Determine ongoing meeting times and locations (typically three hours per week, but can be up to a full day at a time for larger projects). Review discovery assignments for next meeting
- Closing comments around the table: What are your thoughts about the project we are embarking on?

During Phase 1, we want to make sure that group members understand what they are going to be working on—the tasks—and something about the people they will be working with. During team forming, team members internally size each other up and form initial opinions about each other.

Here are a few more details about this first team meeting. When the group meets for the first time the project sponsor goes over situation summary and scope. The project owner goes over deliverables, project phases, and resources described in the whitepaper and then both leaders engage the team in a discussion about the white paper and the project. By the end of this discussion, team members are clear about what they will be working on and the results they should achieve.

The team facilitator takes over to begin the forming work, which will help group members create a team identity and connect to the project. The facilitator reviews the Co-Create model, including the six phases and four big ideas, to give the participants an overview of their purpose and path. This is done in four rounds—one for each big idea. The discussion must be participative and engaging, not just a review of information. Depending on the project this information might be recorded on a flip chart or in the meeting notes. Here are some typical questions we have team members discuss about the four big ideas:

- **We are here to serve something greater than ourselves**: How does this principle specifically relate to this project? How might we define something greater for this project?
- **We are connected and interdependent—existing in complex systems**: Who are the stakeholders connected to this project? What is at stake for each? What connections and partnerships will be needed to succeed? How are various project stakeholders connected and what expectations might they have for the team because of these relationships? How well has the relationship worked in the past?
- **Doubts**: What doubts or concerns do you have about this work? What are the forces driving this project forward? What barriers do you see to saying yes to this work? What's at risk? What crossroads are we at? How will this change affect you?
- **We are here to contribute gifts**: What gifts are you bringing to this project? What gifts do you see around the table? Are there other gifts we may need to accomplish the work? For example, we use a Gifts Discussion Guide, Example 4.1 shown in the following, to help team members identify and share their unique gifts. This is also an opportunity to discuss other personality assessment if they are available. Tools such as Insight Discovery, Myers-Briggs, PI, and DISC are helpful.

Example 4.1

Co-Create—Gifts Discussion Guide

Please think about what you are bringing to this work.

1. Knowledge:
   - I have specific knowledge and experience with this process or issue.
   - I have experience in another setting (company, outside organization) that will be helpful.
   - I have formal education or training that will be helpful.
   - I have considerable experience and knowledge of this business model.
2. Soft skills:
   - Analyze and solve problems
   - Make sound decisions
   - Innovate
   - Establish plans
   - Manage execution
   - Influence others
   - Build relationships
   - Display organizational savvy
   - Manage disagreements
   - Prepare written communication
   - Act with integrity
   - Commit to quality
   - Focus on customer needs
3. Technical skills:
   - I am highly skilled in the following software packages: Word, PowerPoint, Excel, Visio, or Other.

These questions will come back into consideration in later project phases as team members build their understanding of the work and each other. In addition, the team facilitator will use these questions to help the team if it gets off track or loses momentum.

For Individuals—Sensing–Redirecting

During Phase 1, individual team members seek to reduce the natural ambiguity that comes with a new project launch. By engaging in the project and process review meetings, they will build an understanding of the need for change and the implications for them personally. Our goal is that each team member feels committed, comfortable, and clear about his or her path forward. But before that occurs, it sometimes begins with some discomfort. We ask team members to think about:

- How will this change affect you?
- Specifically what part(s) of your job may need to be done differently?
- Will any of your key relationships be impacted?
- What are your personal pluses or minuses? Will life become better, worse or no different?

At this stage it's more important to ask these questions than to get definitive answers. It may be too early for the person to know or they may need to think about it. On the individual level this is about opening up the thought process.

Pitfalls to Avoid

It is important to take the time to adequately define the project. Don't skimp on the amount of analysis and description you do to prepare a great white paper. It is also important to engage team members in a thorough review of the white paper and the Co-Create model. Time spent now is an investment.

Considerations for Leaders

Leaders are often project owners or sponsors and thus play a big role during Phase 1 of the Co-Create model. Help ensure that each project is adequately defined and resourced. Then take the time to share the back story—the "whys" behind the need and context for the change. Be available and eager to engage the team in dialogue.

Conclusion

The team is ready to move on to Phase 2 when as a result of this participation the following are complete: the white paper has been completed, reviewed, the sponsor has committed the resources to complete the project, and the team is clear about their objectives and roles.

Output Example—The White Paper

Here are several short excerpts from a white paper from a successful project. You will notice that this whitepaper retains the style and individual tone of the project owner. This is typical and desired. We want white papers to contain helpful information that is both factual and emotional. You will find another example of a white paper in Addendum C.

Project Name: Database Publishing

Defining Database Publishing

Although database publishing (DBP) significantly impacts the production of all catalogs, this document will address the effect on the full line. DBP can best be described as the effective throughput of data from merchandising through publishing. Since "data" is the key word, it is only fitting that DBP packages are a collection of relational databases, which fully integrate all the elements used in analyzing and publishing catalogs.

Purpose

DBP will create tools for merchandising, direct marketing, and advertising to produce catalogs more efficiently. This will allow Hubert to respond quickly to market change and position itself for future trending of smaller runs and variable printing. These changes are projected to reduce throughput and possibly personnel (or increase capacity) by quicker page assembly, less proofing (mistakes) stages, less copy and price input, and faster and more accurate analysis of pages.

Situational Summary

A Hubert goal is to create partnerships with customers by anticipating their needs. An intimacy with the customer is enhanced through meeting these needs both fully and timely. Important factors in becoming more intimate include: (a) the development of custom catalogs specifically designed for them; (b) quick implementation of custom programs; and (c) the assembly and offering of the right products for that customer.

Typical DBP Changes Include:

1. A centralized storage of copy/text for multiple uses with immediate availability, which can be easily edited and entered only once. This drastically cuts down on human error and enhances continuity. Additionally, copy may be custom written for specific customers and stored and quickly retrieved for multiple uses.
2. A centralized storage of images for multiple uses and immediate availability, which can be easily maintained, but more importantly, viewed by all users.
3. A centralized price table, which is easily maintained and downloaded. This will eliminate up to six price entries.
4. A centralized document management distribution database provides process integrity.
5. Analytical tools for merchandising, which will give them quicker, easier, and more accurate information about product, presentation, page sales, and profit data.

Project Process (Objectives)

- The first objective for Hubert was to document the existing literature development process from concept through delivery of files to the printer.
- The second step for Hubert will be to define the optimal workflow. To accomplish this, a team will be assembled with members from each of the key areas: information systems, merchandising, direct marketing, and advertising. This will be a biweekly standing meeting for four weeks.

- The third step will be the refining of job definitions.
- The fourth step will be the development of the request for proposal (RFP).
- The fifth step will be the evaluation of the different proposals.
- The sixth and final step will be the implementation of DBP in conjunction with an outside software vendor.

Scope

Issues covered in this step were:
- Who is responsible for each step?
- What forms are used in the process? Form function? (Accumulated in central binder.)
- Issues yet to be covered, but under way, are:
  - How much time does the process take from beginning to end? (See attached Gantt chart.)
  - What costs are documented in ABC costing for this process? (Reviewing.)
  - What are the bottlenecks in the process? (To be defined in the Optimal Workflow section.)
  - What skills are required to work within this process? (Will partly be defined by DBP vendor.)

Output

This project will establish current performance benchmarks with the expectation for significant reductions or improvements in the following areas:

- Customization and market strengths.
- Reduce cycle time.
- Reduce costs.
- Increase capacity.
- Increase quality and integrity.
- Create better analysis.

CHAPTER 4

Phase 2

Phase 2, *Discovery*, is my favorite part of every project. It is where facts meet perceptions, energy is created, a new perspective and understanding emerges, and the group becomes an effective team. In most projects, team members come together with a valid yet incomplete understanding of the current state. Each person holds his or her understanding with great conviction—it appears to be the "truth." The team facilitator's role is to productively channel the energy as a new "truth" emerges. The underlying feel of this stage is joint learning.

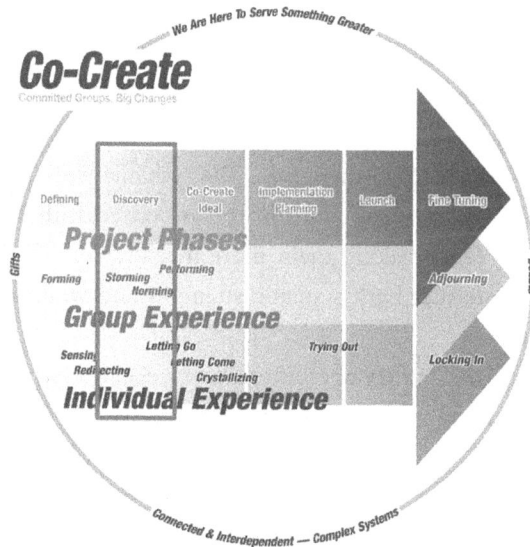

What's Happening at Phase 2?

For the Project—Discovery

The purpose of the discovery phase is to create a complete picture of the current state—the good, bad, and ugly as illustrated by maps, artifacts, and data. The team may take some two to four weeks to pull together an objective representation of the current state. The facilitator utilizes dialogue and analytical tools that help the group collect and understand the information they need.

Once the team identifies the current state, they discuss and describe what's working and what's not working. Typical questions include:

- What is working with the current state that we don't want to lose?
- What about the current state is good but needs adjusting?
- What are the process steps? How are they done?
- Where is the pain? Where do mistakes occur?
- Where does the process take an excessive amount of time?
- Which steps fail to add value?
- What other data do we need to collect and review to have a good understanding? (Cost, time, occurrences, policy or practice, etc.)

It is important here to balance the input between positive and negative. The group will want to talk about all the aspects causing pain. It is human nature to go there first. The systemic weaknesses are only part of the story, however, and may be associated with a well-known failure or problem (making them more memorable). The team facilitator will ensure that both systemic strengths and weaknesses get due consideration.

The team uses a variety of tools to create a detailed picture of the current state including process mapping, affinity diagrams, Pareto diagrams, SWOT (Strengths, Weaknesses, Opportunities, and Threats) analyses, critical pathing, mind maps, and artifacts. The output of this process is often a graphical representation of the discovery information. For projects that don't lend themselves to a graphical presentation it looks like a report. This information is maintained in the meeting space the group is using throughout the project. It provides a touchstone and is a resource to the group throughout the rest of the project.

For the Team—Storming/Norming

Storming and norming (from the Tuckman model of team development, see Chapter 1) team behaviors are normal and tend to show up during every project. The level of team drama experienced is often related to how painful or controversial team members perceive the project. Painful projects are those where two or more departments, or key individuals within these departments, have a history of not working well together, or is the result of controversy when organizational power shifts or roles change. It can also be a function of differing ideas or different styles.

When teams experience conflict or clashes (storming), the facilitator kicks into high gear to create an environment that supports having the tough conversations required to resolve issues while maintaining respectful relationships. Gathering data and mapping processes can be helpful in gaining an objective understanding of the current state. Even so, the underlying emotional issue is sometimes unspoken. The team facilitator helps by asking questions to bring the underlying issue to the surface or by naming the issue. This is commonly known as naming the elephant in the room. For example if *listening for understanding* was identified as a group norm during the forming stage the facilitator makes sure that it is followed as the project unfolds. If the facilitator sees a situation where one team member is not allowing another to express their thoughts then the facilitator should call that out and stop the conversation. The facilitator can tie it back to the initial norms to validate the reason for stopping. The facilitator would then redirect the conversation allowing the person who was not listened to have their say—demonstrating the desired behavior. The situation becomes a teachable moment for the group to calibrate what the norm actually looks like in practice.

When issues are candidly discussed the team grows together. The energy shifts—the conversation becomes authentic and heartfelt with the individuals and the group moving into a different state of being. Productive storming and norming team work sets the stage for the performing phase.

By the end of this phase the past has been discussed and acknowledged; disagreements have been surfaced and discussed from both perspectives;

group members "see" the other side, although they may not agree. Team members trust each other enough to move forward.

For Individuals—Letting Go

The group and individual work is tightly intertwined during this phase of the Co-Create model. Team conversations during storming and norming typically deal with personal feelings, opinions, preferences, and relationship history. A great facilitator will ensure that each employee is able to tell his or her story, share perspectives, and feel heard. When we tell our story, we are able to express and deal with our doubts, concerns, and hopes. One of my favorite questions to ask the team at this phase is, "what do we need (as a group and individually) to let go of in order to create something better?" Our preferred approach is to handle the storming in the group context. If for some reason that breaks down we will end an unproductive exchange and reach out to people individually to explore issues and work on a resolution. The facilitator might readdress the issue at the next meeting or not— depending on the situation.

Pitfalls to Avoid

Silence and agreement are often not the same things. A team might be storming under the surface. They will not be able to do their best work unless unresolved issues are dealt with. The team facilitator and project owner must work together to bring issues to the surface so they can be addressed. The last thing you want is for an unresolved issue to cause problems in a later phase.

Considerations for Project Owners

Encourage an open and candid discussion of the current state. If teams cannot be "real," you will not achieve the best results. Ensure that your actions or decisions don't inadvertently encourage the status quo or an unrealistic view of how things work (or don't work) in your organization.

Also, expect that all teams will go through some storming and show your support.

Conclusion

The team is ready to move on to Phase 3 when they have created a detailed description of the current state and have dealt with any initial teaming issues to the satisfaction of the project owner and facilitator. The output is graphical in form and is key to getting people to a common understanding. Once this work is done, they "get it." We often bring the sponsor in at this point to share what the team has learned. No one comes into the project with the full picture and this process enables discovery that is very useful.

> *"Work can be one of the most joyful, most fulfilling aspects of life. Whether it will be or not depends on the actions we collectively take."*
> —Mihaly Csikszentmihalyi

Output Example—The 32-Foot Process Map

Here is a summary of what one team did during Phase 2. This was a labor of love and perseverance and took the team four weeks to complete. The work was well worth the time invested as it allowed them to have a common and complete understanding of the current state. This understanding provided the foundation needed to create a solution that worked.

Project Name: Database Publishing

What We Did

- Key stakeholders told us what they did.
- Painstaking detail.
- 300 tasks defined.
- More than 1,000 pages of exhibits.
- 32-feet of wall space.
- Paper, electronic, nondocumented, intuitive, in the mind— we documented it all.

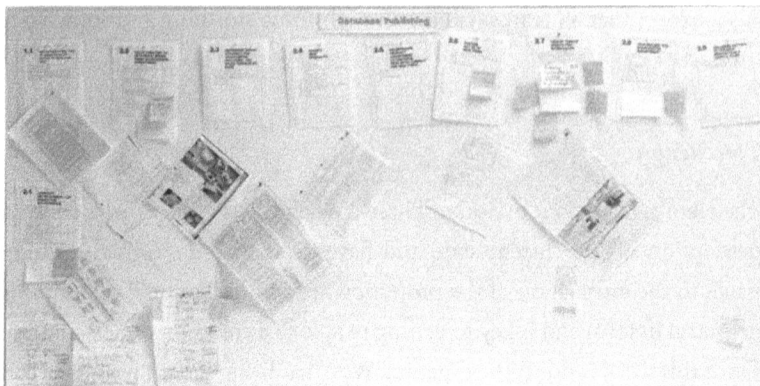

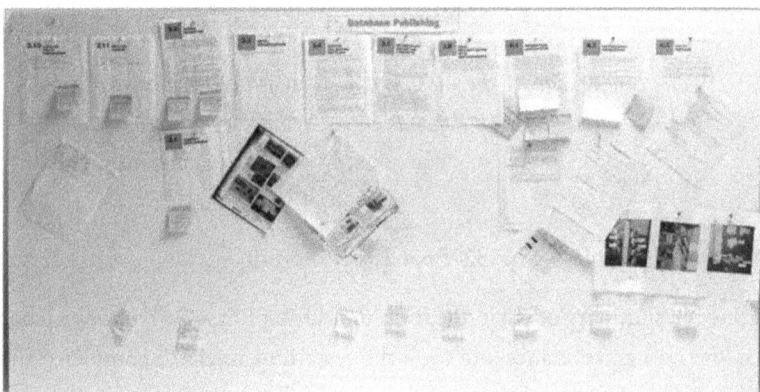

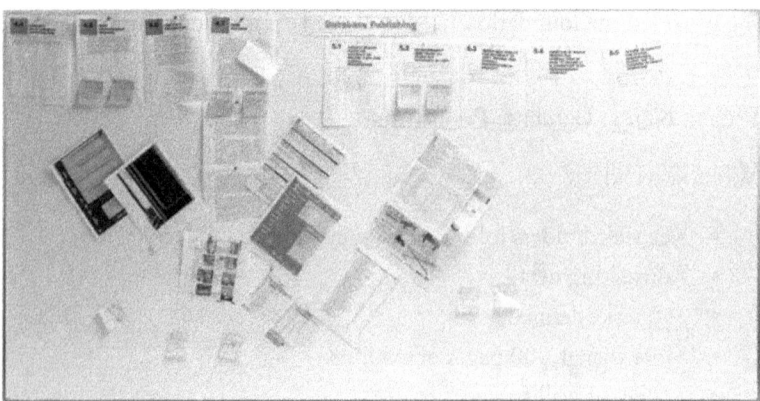

CHAPTER 5

Phase 3

Phase 3, *Co-Create the Ideal*, is where new possibilities emerge. All the prior work—defining a meaningful project, assembling the right group of people, doing the discovery work to understand the current state completely, and working through the emotional stuff—has positioned the group to co-create something great. The team facilitator has an important role to play and it begins with using questions to frame the next phase of work.

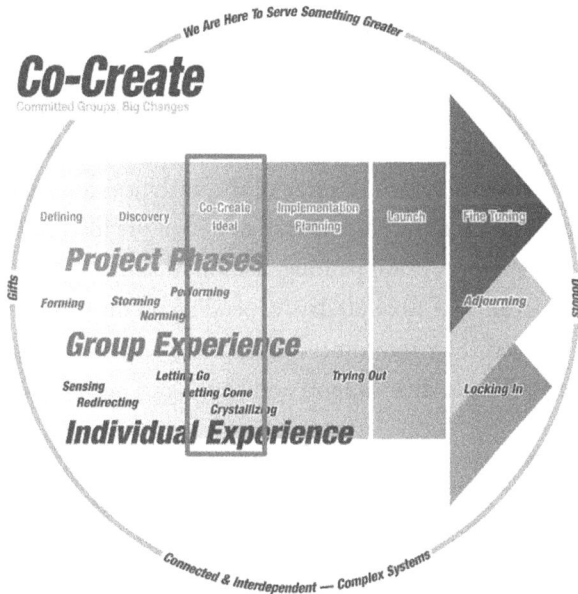

What's Happening at Phase 3?

For the Project—Co-Create the Ideal

The objective of this phase is to create a new product or way of working—to define the ideal change that satisfies the desired outcomes of the project.

The potential solution the team creates could be a brand new workflow, new structure, new guideline, new software, or even a new product strategy. Before starting, the team ensures their focus by reviewing their project objectives and deliverables as expressed in the whitepaper. And the team facilitator will walk the team through a review of the current state to ensure that they are ready to co-create. To begin, the team explores and answers questions such as:

- Ideally, what would accomplish our objectives?
- What might the ideal process look like?
- What do we want to create together?
- What needs to be different?
- What don't we want to lose?

The team facilitator captures the information as the group begins to work. A blank whiteboard turns into a detailed solution as evidenced by new maps, workflows, artifacts, and other documents. The team's work session notes, documented on whiteboards or flip charts, are messy and voluminous. Accurately capturing the information is critical and a challenge. The team may return to some of the analytical tools they used in Phase 2 to understand the current state to design the ideal future including process mapping, critical pathing, and mind maps.

This work can take 30 to 60 days depending on the project. Once the team has defined their recommended approach, they share it with the project sponsor to get their support and blessing to move forward.

For the Team—Performing

Phase 3 requires the team to work well together. It is important that storming and norming issues are worked out before getting to this part of the project. I have found that the data generation processes in Phase 2 enable team members to get to know each other and help them work through many of their concerns.

The team facilitator will structure team processes to bring out everyone's ideas. This serves the project outcome and the team. During the performing phase of team development, ideas come from many team members and spawn new and creative approaches. Group interactions help move things forward, and mutual respect and energy are high.

For Individuals—Sensing-Letting Come/Crystallizing

New ideas become apparent on the individual level and are expressed in the group. This step can be overwhelming as it sometimes is a challenge to process all the new ideas. Minor personal doubts or concerns may still be present although most team members will feel willing to move forward. If the facilitator senses that significant unexpressed doubts or concerns are present they may elect to ask the group directly for their thoughts. If that does not work it may require some one-on-one work outside the meeting to explore the concern.

Many team members feel a sense of accomplishment when they get to the point of creating a tangible solution. One of the most significant outcomes of this stage is that it creates commitment and accountability. *We tend to commit to solutions we create.* This commitment is important for two reasons. First, the individuals on the team will be involved in training or communicating the change to the rest of the organization. Peer endorsement has tremendous credibility with the frontline staff. Secondly, implementing a significant change has some ups and downs. A committed individual will figure out the necessary adjustments needed to make the project a success.

Facilitators check in with team members a lot as they work through the process, and always at the end of each meeting. Example questions for this process check include:

- How are you feeling about the solution we've come up with?
- Do you feel it will accomplish the objectives?
- In two words give me your evaluation of our work today.

These questions can spawn great conversations as individuals and team members process the work. It helps crystallize or move a thought forward.

Pitfalls to Avoid

The most common pitfall during this phase occurs when we don't give the group permission or encouragement to think broadly—it is important that divergent thinking occurs before converging on a solution.

Our facilitators also need to ensure that the focus on task achievement (coming up with a great idea) does not take their attention off what's happening within the team. Ideas are important things to people. We do not want to inadvertently allow team members to feel disrespected or devalued.

The facilitator has to do a great job capturing and documenting information. This is best done at the end of the meeting while it is still fresh in the facilitator's mind. It also includes working the data—taking the messy flipcharts and notes and getting them into presentable form. This can take a number of steps with the group reviewing what was captured and evaluating it for completeness or accuracy.

Considerations for Project Owners

This is the phase of the Co-Create model where project owners need to ensure that their actions and words communicate that they trust the process. It is easy to advocate opinions and ideas in ways that squelch the team's creativity. It is also important that leaders encourage bold thinking and allow the team the time it takes to get beyond the most obvious answers. Even if the team ends up recommending one of their early ideas, the process they go through to consider more alternatives will serve the project outcomes well.

Conclusion

The team is ready to move on to Phase 4 when a defined and agreed-to solution has been achieved. The team should be a high performing unit and individuals should feel valued and ready to contribute their best efforts for the implementation phases of the project.

"Only by engaging can you influence. But engaging also means you will be influenced." Peter Firestein

Output Example:

This image depicts an ideal process map. The top row documents the workflow while the artifacts below add clarity. We prefer this informal approach over creating a digital visual because team members can easily come up to the board and add or move things around. If you work with virtual teams, you will want to find a software program that creates this same inviting dynamic.

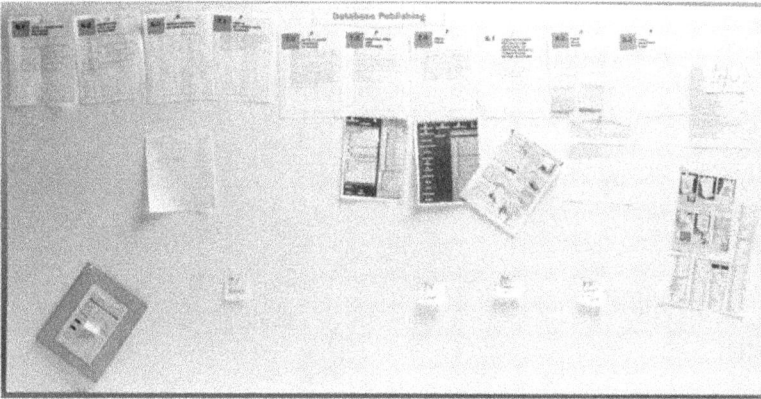

CHAPTER 6

Phase 4

Phase 4, *Implementation Planning*, is the stage where the team defines and clarifies the actions required to make the work a reality. Questions focus on what the team needs to do to execute the project and get the desired results. The team facilitator helps capture and organize ideas and guide the group.

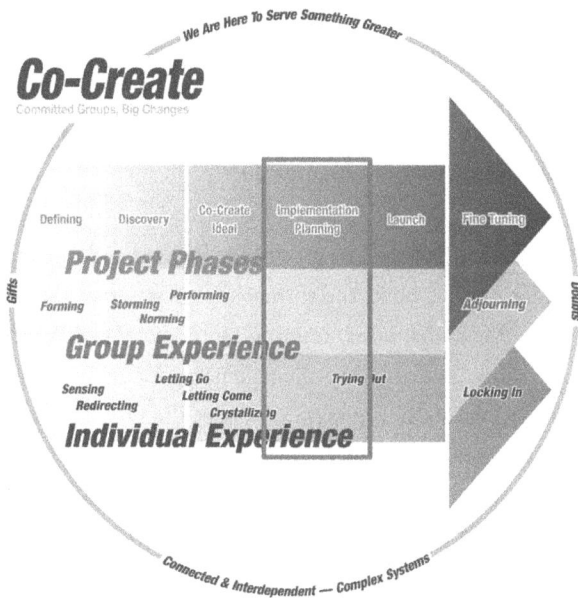

What's Happening at Phase 4?

For the Project—Implementation Planning

During Phase 4, the team deepens and refines their project plan and communicates progress to leaders. Updates include information about who is doing what, measures of progress, and any changes or adjustments that will be required to complete the project. Questions that the team explores include:

- What supporting information is needed on the frontline level? How will it be accessed? How will it be kept up-to-date?
- What changes will managers or others need to make?
- Do we need to modify our software to support the changes?
- How will the managers manage this change?
- Does this change affect the performance management system (changes to responsibility or performance standards)? Is this change significant enough to affect compensation?
- What do we need to communicate to stakeholders?
- What will the implementation training look like? Who will develop the materials and present?
- When will the new software be ready? Do we need to pilot this change before rolling it out to the organization?
- Do we have any policy issues that should be discussed with the project sponsor or executives?

The team facilitator helps the group stay focused and moving forward. The team's plan should be in the format that best serves the project and could include charts, diagrams, training materials, PowerPoint presentations, screen shots, performance management documents, organization charts, or other materials. The team produces the type and level of detail needed to implement the project through to affected stakeholders. The individuals and groups who need to execute the change should have all the information and training required to do it.

For the Team—Performing

At this stage the group is highly productive. Group process issues have been resolved. Team members understand their role and the gifts others are providing to the project. Information and help is readily exchanged between team members. Individuals volunteer to work on tasks outside their to-do lists. Solutions are quickly developed to problems as they arise.

For Individuals—Trying Out

While some residual doubt may remain, new behaviors are practiced and learned. Team members test methods offline or as part of a pilot program.

Pitfalls to Avoid

It is important to allow the team adequate time to think through implementation details and considerations. It is tempting to rush into launching once we have agreed upon a solution. The implementation plan must take all parts of the system into consideration.

Considerations for Project Owners

For leaders, this is where the rubber meets the road in terms of support. Make sure that you clearly understand how users and stakeholders will be impacted, any training they will need, and their roles in the implementation of the change. Is the implementation plan realistic? Take time to understand the details and ensure that the plan will produce the desired changes.

Conclusion

The team is ready to move on to Phase 5 when they have created a detailed implementation plan, required materials, and documents needed to launch the change to the individual user level.

Output Example:

During Phase 4, the team completed the following:

- Created a detailed document connecting the steps in the workflow with the use of the software.
- Partnered with the training and development team to plan and conduct the training.

- Created a training model that specifically outlined, by user group, the training they would need to get up to speed. The training was sequenced for optimal effectiveness.
- Installed and tested the software in preparation for the training and the "go live" date.

CHAPTER 7

Phase 5

During the *launch* phase, the team implements the project and begins seeing results. All the development work is complete—the necessary documents have been created, the software written and tested, the necessary updates with the project sponsor are accomplished. The project goes "live."

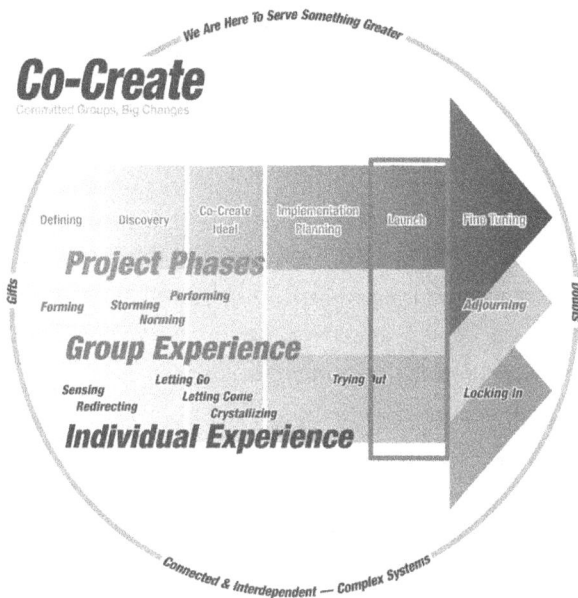

What's Happening at Phase 5?

For the Project—Launch

During this phase of the Co-Create model, team members conduct the training or implement the communication plan with all stakeholder groups. They act as go-to people for questions and answers, keep an eye on how the implementation is going, and address any unanticipated issues or unintended consequences. The team meets to discuss progress and course corrections, but only as needed (they no longer have weekly meetings).

For the Team—Performing

Team members co-deliver training and present a cohesive cross-functional front. They are using inclusive language demonstrating ownership. Like a proud artisan they generate positive energy for the change and act as ambassadors for the work that needs to be done. They listen and gather important information from users to feed the fine tuning phase.

For Individuals—Trying Out

Since team members are often also users they are actively using the new approach, tools, or work process. This is an important source of fine tuning information and also reinforces their credibility with their peers.

Pitfalls to Avoid

The most common pitfall we've experienced at this phase of the project is failing to spend the time needed to help team members prepare to communicate the change and conduct training programs. They must be comfortable and prepared since the credibility of the solution could be negatively impacted by lousy training. The team facilitator works with the team to practice presentations and pilot the training using the team as guinea pigs. The facilitator will also provide individual coaching or partner with the training department to ensure that team members are prepared and confident. Practice sessions also help ensure that the supporting documentation is complete and user friendly.

Considerations for Project Sponsors and Owners

Change occurs when conversations for the change outnumber and outweigh conversations for the old way. Leaders should support the change and improve its success by communicating about the change often. Clarify what's at stake and how this change aligns with the organization's strategies. Encourage open dialogue about the implementation and any setbacks that occur.

Conclusion

The team is ready to move on to the final phase of the Co-Create model once the change plan has been implemented and training or testing has been completed.

CHAPTER 8

Phase 6

During the final stage of the Co-Create model, teams focus on resolving any unanticipated issues and required adjustments. This is the time that they do a post-project review and formally close the project. Given the amount of time and effort expended in previous stages this is an important and quick step.

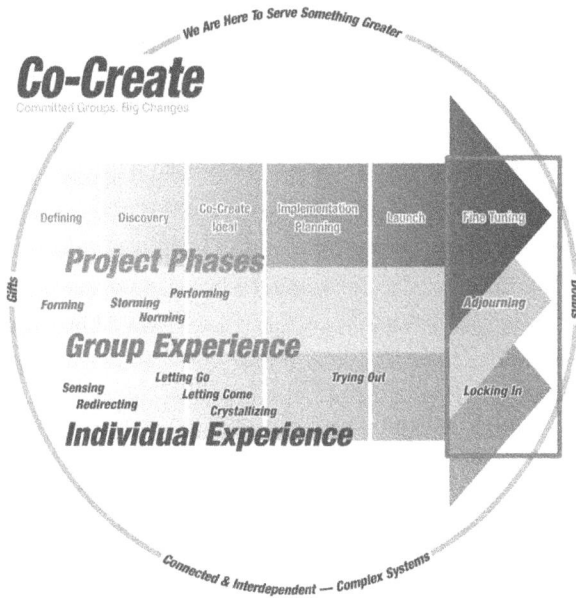

What's Happening at Phase 6?

For the Project—Fine Tuning

Once the team has reached Phase 6, the project is essentially complete. The team will meet one or two more times to ensure that the implementation is complete and to address any additional training needs or requests.

The project owner and sponsor own measuring the impact of the project and reporting results as a part of their regular business update meetings. For example, project owners often report project results at our monthly management meetings and senior leadership business updates.

For the Team—Adjourning

To help the team gain closure, the team facilitator leads a final team meeting where the team discusses their experiences including:

- What went well?
- What did not go well?
- What would you have changed?

These questions cover all three levels of the work—the tasks, the team, and their individual experience. This final meeting moves from post-mortem to a celebration that marks the emotional end of the project.

Our celebrations are held off-site and attended by the project sponsor, the team, and anyone else in the organization that provided support for the project. The sponsor or the team facilitator kicks off the gathering with a few comments that acknowledge the team's results. All participants are given an opportunity to open the floor for anyone else who would like to speak.

For Individuals—Locking In

For the individual, this phase of the project is similar to Phase 5—an emotional high and a few adjustments. This also is the point where, on an individual level they can explore their learning. The facilitator asks:

- What was your biggest learning from this project?
- What one thing would you do different in a future project?

Pitfalls to Avoid

As I mentioned previously, it is important to make sure that you take time to celebrate the ends of a project. The work has been a big emotional and mental challenge and we need to help the team get closure and ensure they feel appreciation for their fine work.

Considerations for Leaders

This is a great opportunity for leaders to recognize the individuals involved and to connect this project back to the big picture. Team members need to know that their efforts made a difference and that upper management sees and values it. The success of this project sets up the next, and the next, and the next project. The team takes the energy and drive (or lack of it) they have at the end of each project into their next assignment. The lessons we learn should benefit future work as well and this is more likely to occur when leaders behave in demonstrably supportive and grateful ways.

Conclusion

The team calls the project complete and many move on to another project on another team. The team facilitator packages up the information and the project owner continues to track and communicate the results.

> *"No man ever steps in the same river twice, for it's not the same river and he's not the same man."*
>
> —Heraclitus

Output Example-Database Publishing Project:

During Phase 6, the team selected the fine tuning group—the best of the best users—as the focal point for the resolution of any outstanding issues and to make final adjustments. Part of their mission was to assess project metrics to see how the implementation was performing. Based on the data the team projected the following annual results for the project:

- Page productivity increase of 42 percent
- Promotional development tasks reduced 33 percent
- Price and copy entered 1× compared to 7× and 4×
- Advertising OT down 65 percent

- Avoided $500,000 in additional capacity expense
- Activity-based costing:
  - $500,00 yearly savings
  - First year "Actual" savings
  - $150,000
  - 300 steps reduced to 200

Conclusion

The Co-Create model helps bring out the best in teams and individuals.

The power of commitment is immense and will change the business when you focus this force on important projects. So where do you go from here? When I talk to colleagues in other companies about this approach, the conversation invariably turns to a discussion of readiness. Here are several questions that can help you determine your organization's readiness for using an integrated team project model like this one.

Is the Organization Ready?

- Is there dissatisfaction in the organization about how projects or change was managed in the past or are people generally happy with your current project management and change methodologies?
- Have there been any recent (or memorable) spectacular project failures or successes?
- Is it difficult to get project teams excited about the work?
- Are key stakeholders happy with the results or would they like to see improvement?
- Are the employees empowered and involved?
- Do employees have the technical and interpersonal skill required to complete great project work?
- Do you have current employee satisfaction data? What does it tell you?

Is the Executive Team Ready?

- Are leaders able to clearly articulate the current state of the business—what's working and what's not?

- Can they translate that into a vision for moving forward including the projects, competencies or changes required to make it happen (at a high level)?
- Are they ready to empower employees to figure out solutions?
- Are they willing to invest the time required for the teams to do it right?
- Are they willing to fund training for the champion to learn the process?
- Are they capable and willing to make tough choices?

Do You have Change Champions?

- Is there someone internally who will champion this work?
- Do they have the necessary skills and influence in the organization?
- Do they see the need for a new way to manage and launch projects and do they have an interest in this work?
- Do they have the time to devote to being a champion?

Answering these questions, and others unique to your situation, will give you a good idea as to whether or not a process like the Co-Create model has application in your organization. While I believe that all organizations will benefit from a strong team-based approach to project management and change, readiness and interest are critical.

The Ready Organization

I am often asked what I believe are the hallmarks of a ready organization. To use an inclusive and integrated approach like Co-Create, an organization needs to have:

1. Competent leadership (sponsors and owners) with a grasp on the real issues and opportunities facing the organization.
2. The ability to translate the issues and opportunities into manageable projects—with enough detail for the group to engage.

3. A functional culture that supports the sharing of power with others. The group working on each project should possess a medium-to-high level of decision-making power.
4. Capable team members—they know their stuff (technical), have the interpersonal skill required to effectively manage differences, and to hold each other accountable. They are willing to accept the challenge.
5. The organization and leaders must have the discipline to give the work the time it needs. The process needs to play itself out.

Here's to Success!

I wish you the best of success and I hope that this information helps you and your peers unleash the talents and potential of your employees and generate great results. What I have discovered is when our beliefs are aligned with how we work, we are able to grow the business and keep all stakeholders—owners, leaders, customers, partners, and employees—engaged and moving forward.

ADDENDUM A

Other Model Elements

As I was writing this book, I was reminded of the many conversations I have had with peers, colleagues, and team facilitators about what makes the Co-Create model stand out and apart from other project management and change models. I have shared several strengths of the model already, but there are more. If you gain nothing else from this book, I hope that you find these elements of the model useful. You can overlay these with your current project management practices and improve results and engagement.

There are six features of the Co-Create model, two of which I have already outlined in the Introduction and earlier chapters. These six differentiating factors support our team culture and improve participation and ownership. They are:

- Tasks, teams, and individuals—our integrated approach as outlined in the Introduction.
- The four big ideas—outlined in Chapter 2.
- Team facilitation—effective facilitation is key to helping team members do their best work.
- Let the team work—trust the process to produce results.
- Visualization—seeing the entire system.
- Flexibility of form—we modify the application of the model to fit the project—not the other way around.

These practices are neither earth shatteringly different nor do they represent a breakthrough in business science. Used together, however, these six methods are powerful. Since I have already written about the first two on the list, integration and the big ideas we'll focus on the latter four here.

Team Facilitation

The team facilitator is not a subject matter expert on the team, but he or she plays a vital role that goes well beyond making sure that meetings have agendas and everyone has a chance to speak. Our facilitators connect deeply so that they can proactively help the team excel in accomplishing tasks, teaming, and individual growth. The facilitator helps ensure the team and individual elements of the Co-Create model are developed as fully and intentionally as they need to be to complete the project.

You will notice that in the coming chapters, I offer specific tasks that the team tackles at each project phase of the model, but fewer that relate to the team or individual tracks. This is because each team is different and every project brings out a different dynamic. The facilitator closely monitors the team's progress and will propose the approaches and tools he or she thinks might help the team the most. With the focus on what's happening in the project phase, the majority of the time is spent there—this group exists to accomplish specific project objectives. That said, the facilitator has the responsibility to intervene as issues or needs surface related to teaming or an individual's contributions. It is a key role for the facilitator.

Does every team need to have a facilitator? Yes, all major projects deserve, and need, a facilitator. By separating this function, we ensure that the facilitator is not encumbered by the temptation to guide the team toward getting to "their" right answer. In the past, we had facilitators who were also team members and this did not work well at all. When facilitators also own a part of the work, they struggle to remain open and fluid. As I mentioned previously, our team facilitators need to attend to the team and individual dynamics and not be sidetracked by other interests.

In addition to ensuring team and team member engagement, the facilitator helps the team create visual representations of their work throughout the project. They ensure that our sense of urgency or competing demands don't result in shortcuts to the crucial exploration and definition aspects of the work. I will discuss the importance of our visual approach in the following.

Our team development process is experiential, versus training, driven. What I mean by this is that our teams learn how to be great teams by experience with the model. For example the team facilitator will help team members become better listeners in the course of team meetings and by having open discussions about the quality of their discussions. We help them work better together by facilitating conversations where they work things out.

To accomplish all these outcomes our facilitators need to be open, at times courageous, and driven to make teams better. Our team facilitator training process emphasizes the tools, practices, and beliefs that we know will help our teams succeed. The training program generally takes about a week to complete. The final six sessions are all skill-based training—the participants are up in front of the group getting experience and receiving feedback. Ideally the group size is six to eight with two trainers.

The components are:

1. How to conduct an orientation and planning session.
2. A deep review of the Co-Create model.
3. How to write a whitepaper and how to coach project owners (we devote an entire session to this topic).
4. Introduction to facilitation skills that cover our three project dimensions—the work, the team, and individuals.
5. How to help groups make effective decisions.
6. Creating commitment and participation.
7. Managing group conflict.
8. Facilitating effective meetings.
9. Using the core data gathering, organizing, and analysis tools.
10. Facilitating implementation planning and next steps.

It is an involved process teaching a complex task. We tell all our participants that doing this work is somewhat of an adventure. The good news is that they have a map of the territory and a good set of tools to work with. The bad news is that no two projects are alike and the actual terrain always contains differences from the map. What's required is for the facilitator to use their best judgment about what to do next as the adventure unfolds. In many ways it's best described as a practice—one with a body of knowledge associated with it, but requiring constant adjustment. The only way to build your team facilitation skills is to do it over and over again.

Let the Team Work

The project owner is a project team member—not a team leader. The team should not *immediately* defer to him or her for decisions. We work hard, with the help of the team facilitator, to ensure that the team does not feel overly influenced by the project owner. I realize that this might seem odd to you because the project owner, after all, OWNS the project.

I can remember one project owner who apparently viewed the Co-Create model as a great tool for getting everything HE wanted done. He had the solution figured out before the first meeting. This intention quickly became apparent to the group and they shut down. The team felt the project was "rigged" and that the owner was asking for their input when in reality he didn't really want it. The team saw the truth—it was an act of manipulation not engagement. Yes, our teams accomplish great things, but every project must unfold naturally and generatively. We talked with him about our team approach and that although the project owner and sponsor draw up an initial scope and definition for each project in the white paper (Phase 1), the team then takes over to shape and execute the project together. Ultimately, this particular leader was not a good fit for our organization's culture and he moved on.

The relationship between project owners and project teams runs two ways—both serve the other, both lead. The trick is in knowing when to lead and when to follow or collaborate. We have had project owners who needed to make adjustments to how they approached the team and how they participated as a team member. Our team facilitators are trained to spot potential issues and coach owners on how to prevent getting in the way of team progress.

The benefits of trust go beyond projects as well. Our managers learn how to lead in ways that open up and tap into talent. And they learn that although they often have great ideas about how projects ought to be completed, the team can and will consider more ideas, uncover more potential root causes, and create even better solutions that they are fully committed to.

The Power of Visuals

You will see a couple of examples of our huge "as is" process maps. One diagram was 32 feet long and wrapped around several conference room walls! Many organizations use process mapping, mind mapping, and other visual analysis methods. The idea is not new, but perhaps you might find our approach helpful.

Our teams go big and deep with the visuals they create and we do not short-change the time it takes to get to the most meaningful level of understanding. It would be easy for a team to rationalize spending less time and taking less effort to map out project processes if most in the room thought they already had a clear understanding of it. Our experience tells us that what we think we understand is different than what we really understand.

Visual representations improve our understanding and increase team member buy-in. Seeing is believing and until we take the time to sketch out a solution or connect the dots within a complex process, we can't fully move forward. The time is well spent. Figure A.1 shows an example from the discovery phase of a project where we redesigned our assortment management process. On the left, we mapped the current workflow and indicated specific pain points with the starbursts. The team also gathered artifacts representing the different reports and documents (along with the system that generated it) that are used to support the decision making involved in this process. This exercise helped the team see that accessibility and availability of information was a major barrier. This then set up the next phase, Co-Create the Ideal, where a completely new software solution was created to make the information available in real time, in one place, and down to the detail needed by the merchants. The team created this visual over two meetings, with individuals working on certain pieces of it outside the meetings.

Visual analysis also improves team development. Everyone gets involved and the room feels electric. Team members are up at the boards adding content and pointing to areas of conflict—it introduces a physical connection to the work (see Figure A.1). This increases retention and understanding. When posted on the wall or on a screen, these visuals prompt better discussions and questions and clearly reveal gaps, overlaps, inadequacies, and new possibilities. They also live on in the conference room where the group is meeting for the duration of the project. This is valuable because it provides a touchstone—it is easily accessed to review or remind the group about some aspect of the data.

Visual Analysis Graphic

Whether you fully implement the Co-Create model or not, I recommend you allow ample time for your project teams to go big and deep with visual tools. This practice benefits the work and the team relationships.

Flexible Form

I am often asked about the templates we use for the various tasks that teams complete throughout the six phases of the Co-Create model. Many have seemed surprised with my answer. We have very few templates at all and, in fact, resist requesting standard forms, templates, or standard outlines.

Each team decides how they want to analyze, document, measure, and communicate their work with the facilitators' guidance. Their approaches are based on the project, the team, and the situation. For example, the

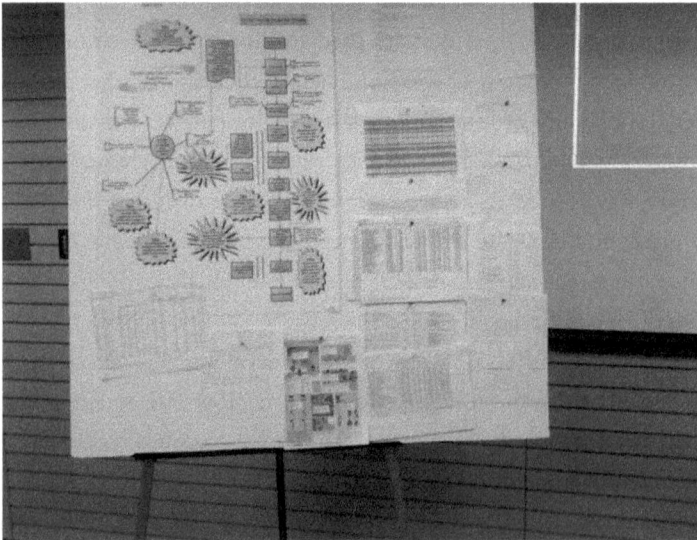

Figure A.1 Visual analysis example

white paper for one project looked like a marketing brochure while other teams have used simple text or presentation formats. The points they cover are similar (see Chapter 4) but the included information can and does vary.

We focus on the quality of the work, period. If the team is doing their best work and if tasks, roles, measures, and outcomes are clear, why should we micromanage their work processes and products? Some people argue that having a template will save time and help teams be more efficient. We believe that there is little value in requiring teams to use certain formats for their work, dictating HOW tasks are done would violate our underlying beliefs. It would be inconsistent for us to tell our teams that they own creating and launching this project, but that report needs to look a certain way. To create a strong culture, we need to walk our talk with our purpose and beliefs.

This approach, like others I have shared, has a positive impact on project-related work. We are driven by results, not formality. Our flexible work practices have improved employee engagement and ownership.

Considerations for Leaders

The six differentiating factors of the Co-Create model come together to create the "secret sauce" of our approach. Our leaders not only support these approaches, they own them. And this is an important point of distinction. The "trust in the process" idea, for example, is hollow and meaningless unless leaders believe that this is the right way to work and they show it through consistent words, actions, and decisions.

Conclusion

This is the essence of the Co-Create model and what makes it both unique and incredibly effective. When I think about the results we get from our project teams, I am amazed. But then I remember the power of these approaches and the talent and dedication of our team members and facilitators and it all makes perfect sense. For our team members, it is considered a good thing to work on a project because they know they are helping to change and improve the business.

In the coming chapters, you will see how these differentiators are manifested throughout the six phases of the model. The bottom line is that if you select the right ones, a few changes can make a big difference and help your teams work and relate at a higher level.

"If we're growing we're always going to be out of our comfort zone"

—John Maxwell

ADDENDUM B

About Commitment

Presented here is the background information from some really smart people who have written about commitment both from a team and general leadership perspective.

For anyone who has lead or worked on a team, there is a night and day difference if the team is highly committed to accomplishing its goal. With a highly committed team there is focus, energy, and a feeling that nothing will stop them from getting to the goal. To experience that is to be part of something special. If commitment is lacking the experience is painful on many fronts. So what is the difference? What do we know about commitment, engagement, and the human experience of working collaboratively? And more importantly, is there anything a leader can do to create the environment for commitment to flourish. Fortunately the answer is yes.

Employee commitment, engagement, and empowerment have been part of the leadership conversation for some time. This topic has received considerable attention because the general level of employee engagement in the United States has been estimated to be about 33 percent. I'm not aware of any research specifically focused on project team engagement but I believe it's safe to assume that there is considerable room for improvement. I will review some key learning from highly regarded thought leaders and discuss how a project manager or leader can improve the level of engagement and commitment of a team.

Let's start at the beginning—what is a team and what role does team commitment play?

Jon R. Katzenbach and Douglas K. Smith wrote a seminal book on teams called *The Wisdom of Teams*. Their definition is:

"A team is a small number of people with complementary skills who are **committed** to a common purpose, performance goals, and approach for which they hold themselves mutually accountable." (Pg. 41)

Jon R. Katzenbach and Douglas Smith, *The Wisdom of Teams*, Harvard Business Review Press, Boston, 1993.

In examining their model, graphically depicted in the following, you can see that *commitment* is the foundation with skills and accountability enabled by a meaningful purpose, common approach, and specific goals. Without commitment the house has no foundation and it becomes unlikely that the team will succeed. A meaningful purpose addresses the "why" of the work with a common approach the "how" and specific goals the ultimate measure of success. In my experience, if a sponsor or project manager addresses these three items as part of the kick-off session most likely they are presenting this information with the team largely passive. Gaining commitment is not a passive process. I'll talk later about how to do this differently to greatly increase the level of commitment.

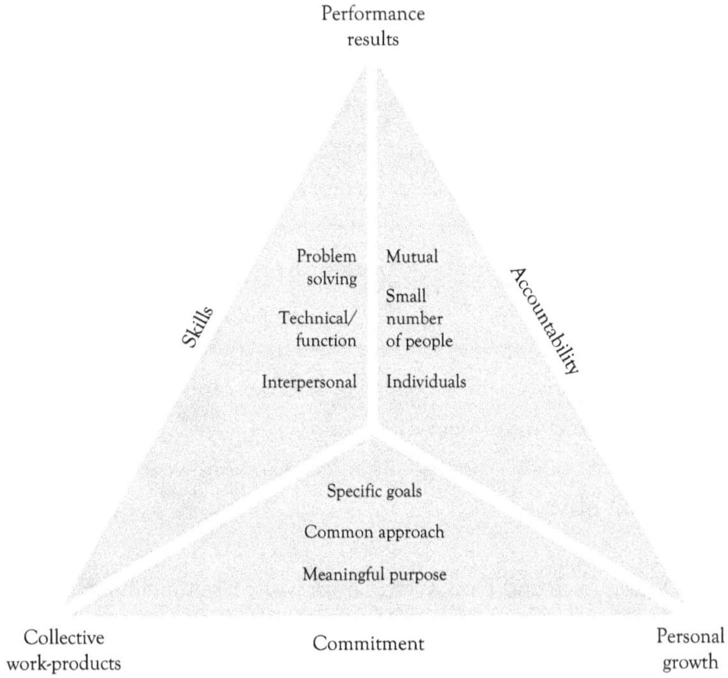

Performance
results

Problem
solving   Mutual

Small
Technical/   number
function   of people

Interpersonal   Individuals

Skills

Accountability

Specific goals

Common approach

Meaningful purpose

Collective
work-products   Commitment   Personal
growth

Figure B.1 Katzenbach and Smith team model

Patrick Lencione, a highly regarded management consultant and author, has written extensively about teams. In his New York Times best seller, *The Five Dysfunctions of a Team*, Lencione states that team dysfunction is comprised of the following components:

1. Absence of trust
2. Fear of conflict
3. *Lack of commitment*
4. Avoidance of accountability
5. Inattention to results

All five are connected and unfold from the top down. The dysfunction begins with a lack of trust among team members. Without the ability for team members to engage in authentic conversation it becomes impossible to build trust. Without trust a fear of conflict surfaces—team members can't be sure of where others are coming from or if they have ulterior motives. It becomes a very political environment, which ultimately creates a corrosive group environment where self-interest becomes more important than serving the greater good.

He also talks extensively about what trust looks like in practice.

The kind of trust that is necessary to build a great team is what I call *vulnerability-based trust*. This is what happens when members get to a point where they are completely comfortable being transparent, honest, and naked with one another, where they say and genuinely mean things like "I screwed up," "I need help," "Your idea is better than mine," "I wish I could learn to do that as well as you do," and even "I'm sorry."

At the heart of vulnerability lies the willingness of people to abandon their pride and their fear, to sacrifice their egos for the collective good of the team. (Pg. 27)

And finally:
Achieving commitment:

People will not actively commit to a decision if they have not had the opportunity to provide input, ask questions, and understand the rationale behind it. Another way to say this is, "If people don't weigh in, they can't buy in." (Pg. 48)

Lenciones' prescription is clear…for teams to be effective the "soft stuff" must be actively attended to. A leader is responsible to *lead by example*—creating a supportive environment for the team. It's then up to each individual on the team to have the courage to be vulnerable—to push through the discomfort and connect.

Patrick Lencioni, *The Advantage: Why Organizational Health Trumps Everything Else in Business*, Jossey-Bass, 2012.

Peter Block, Flawless Consulting, 3rd Edition

Peter Block has also written extensively about how a leader can authentically connect with team members. He stresses that the leader's task is to demonstrate or model authenticity and openness in every interaction with the team. This begins at the very first meeting. He writes…

To open a conversation or gathering, describe the concerns that began the process, define where the change effort is at this moment, describe what the organization needs from us right now, and give some idea of the structure of this step.

Most of us are familiar with the need for this kind of information. **The key is to tell the whole story**. This includes weaknesses and failure. Don't protect people from the bad news in the name of protecting them from anxiety. Anxiety is a natural state, best handled in the light of day. The only caution is to keep it short and informal, with more from the heart than head. (Pg. 263)

The beginning of a project is the best time to get the team members involved and active. The opportunity is to have a real, complete conversation about the work ahead. Every major project has inherent in it positives and negatives. To present only the upside smacks of manipulation to those around the table. A mistake leaders often make is to avoid discussing anything negative so as not to poison the project from the beginning or that someone will bring up an issue that has no ready answer. Unfortunately by not presenting a complete picture the audience is left with the feeling that they are being sold. Block writes:

> Human systems are not so orderly, and many doubts go unanswered. In creating high engagement, it is the expression of doubt that counts, not its resolution. We cannot construct a plan that eliminates all doubts, but we can always acknowledge them. We can acknowledge cynicism and make room for it without being paralyzed by it. The fact that the most alienated people in the organization are given a platform to speak does more to build commitment from those watching the conversation than any compelling presentation or financial incentive program ever can. (Pg. 267)

Commitment is ultimately chosen by each individual team member. It cannot be mandated nor bought. This judgment is an emotional one—it drives off of the feeling we have as a result of the interaction with the team leader and members. If transparency, authenticity, and openness are not encouraged and reinforced, commitment will suffer. It takes courage and self-awareness to step into this conversation and through the discomfort. If one makes the effort the rewards are great.

Too often our interactions with project teams come from a compliance perspective. We revert back to the expectation that people on the team are being paid to do a job and should follow through with energy and excellence. This transactional perspective leaves no place for commitment...nor does it address the human emotions that are fundamental to exceptional performance. Commitment by its very nature is emotional—it speaks to a psychological bond to a project, the team members, and the organization. It's our job as project leaders to not lose sight of this fact and to make time to address it.

"Seven key features for creating and sustaining commitment," Rachel Burgess and Suzanne Turner, 2000, *International Journal of Project Management*, Pergamon, 225–233.

Burgess and Turner have done a fine job of thinking about how best to create commitment in project teams. They argue that creating commitment is an inside-out job:

> **Commitment** requires the **internalization** of the organizations values, norms, and goals to a point where there is a strong correlation between them and the individuals' beliefs. This level of congruence builds an intense sense of loyalty and dedication, and will make employees both satisfied and productive by their involvement within the organization.

The authors outline seven key features of high commitment:

1. Individuals join of their own free will
   - Members of project teams should have a choice about being part of a project team. If they disagree with the premise or objective they can decline with no repercussions. If they choose to quit after the project is underway there is no road back to this team.
2. The role of uncertainty
   - Uncertainty plays an important role in laying the foundation for change, before the project can begin employees must be freed from their commitment to the past:
     - Nothing stops an organization faster than people who believe that the way they worked yesterday is the best way to work tomorrow. To succeed, not only do your people have to change the way they act, they've got to change the way they think about the past. (24)
       Madonna J., cited in Blanchard K. and Waghorn T., *Mission Possible*, McGraw-Hill, 1997.
     This begins with the business case for change, which is discussed in the opening team meeting.
   - This also affords the team, and each member, the opportunity to create the future organization. This creates a sense of validation that they've been chosen for this important task as well as anxiety—can this be done? Success is not guaranteed. The

anxiety stems from the importance of the task and the possibility that it may not be successful. Failure has both individual as well as organizational implications. Both energies are useful in opening the team up for the creative work to come.

3. Start small and build up

- It's important to have a clear place to start in order for the work to begin successfully. This can be accomplished as the team moves into the initial work of discovery. The short story of discovery is that the project requires each team member to contribute knowledge and perspective about the current state. This typically proves to be very affirming because they share their expertise with the group. This begins to form the team as people share and others get a sense of the contributions and talent on the project team.

4. Joining requires individual effort

- Being part of this project comes with a very real challenge and cost. Most projects have upward visibility—either to higher functional levels or in some cases to the executive team. Participation offers the chance for recognition or a very visible failure—both having potential career implications. Additionally, in mid-size and smaller organization working on a project is in addition to their "regular job"— they have to figure out how to make it all happen successfully. This energy supports commitment.

5. Public acts of commitment

- There is a psychological concept that comes into play that can easily be used by leaders or project managers to help develop commitment. The concept is that we all want to appear to our peers as consistent beings. When our actions and words diverge it creates something called cognitive dissonance. Cognitive dissonance is uncomfortable and human nature is such that we tend to avoid or move away from uncomfortable feelings. Some simple techniques are:
  - ○ When key decisions are made each person should be asked in the team setting…"Are you committed to this decision?"

- Being the "public face" of the project to their functional area for input and ongoing communication.
- Asking individual…"what are you going to do differently?"
- Performing a process check at the end of each team meeting to get their feelings about the project and its current state. This allows an opportunity to express any doubts, concerns, or positive statements about the team's progress. I also often ask the team for any thoughts they have about changes to our process.

The idea is that once a person declares a public position or point of view they will tend to stick with it so as not to appear inconsistent and have to deal with cognitive dissonance or uncomfortable questions from team mates.

6. Active involvement
   - If the team is truly empowered to come up with a solution—they are creating it. Whenever possible team members should be given decision-making ability or authority. Decisions are the ultimate expression of organizational power. The act of deciding results in ownership and commitment.
7. Clear messages and clear lines of communication
   - It's important for the channels to open up, down and sideways. Any impediment to this flow of information or clarity slows the team down and creates frustration.

I'll leave you with a quote from Peter Senge:

> The committed person brings an energy, passion and excitement that cannot be generated if you are only compliant, even genuinely compliant. The committed person doesn't play by the rules of the game. If the rules of the game stand in the way of achieving the vision, he will find ways to change the rules. (5)

Peter Senge, *The Fifth Discipline*, Century Business, 1990.

ADDENDUM C

Change Management Models

As I mentioned in the Introduction, the Co-Create model was inspired by many theorists and practitioners. Each helped shape our thinking and guide decisions about how the model should be used. While there are many other models out there, these have worked for us day in and day out. In this section, I share several of these sources of inspiration and where you can learn more about their work. All of the resources listed in this section are also referenced in the Notes section at the end of the book. Broadly, the influences come from disciplines within behavioral or management sciences:

- Organizational development
- Leadership
- Quality improvement

Kurt Lewin: In the 1940s, Kurt Lewin and his associates developed one of the classic change models. This model frames tasks in understandable terms and is applicable for many types of change—both individual as well as organizational. Lewin breaks change into three parts: unfreezing, change, and refreezing. The first step, unfreezing, speaks to the need for getting ready to change. Using the metaphor of water unfreezing brings to mind a solid structure, ice, needing to change form. If it remains frozen there is not much chance of creating productive change. The best you can do with ice is to break it or put some chemicals on it creating a mess. Unfreezing occurs when we create the case for change and set up the process for moving through it. Done effectively, it provides the rationale for the change. At the end of this stage there may be uncertainty and doubt about what the future holds but there is no doubt about the need to change. During step two we do what's required to make the change, including learning about the current state. Information is gathered from many perspectives. Once a good understanding is achieved, the work of figuring out how to create a better future begins. This work continues until the change is at an implementable stage. The third step, refreezing, is about implementing the change and making it the new norm. This is where new learning occurs, mistakes happen, and new patterns are established. The beauty of Lewin's work is that it provides a basic framework from which to build.

Edgar Schein: Schein built upon Lewin's basic change framework and added additional insights for each of the three stages of change including:

- *Unfreezing*: Schein believes that unfreezing begins with some level of dissatisfaction with the current state. It might be driven by environmental factors, competitors, or new technology, or by a more internal focus—a need that is not being satisfied. Schein believed that once we feel dissatisfied, our psychological reactions will tend to be guilt or anxiety. On the individual level one may feel that they should have anticipated the change or that they have somehow failed. This then creates the anxiety based on the judgments (internal or from others) that may come if change does not occur. This connects directly to self-esteem and beliefs about one's competence. This fear of failure provides a tremendous amount of juice to stimulate action. Schein believed that if guilt or anxiety is too high it inhibits a person's willingness to step out of the current pattern of behavior and take the risk of learning something new—to make the change. A key task of the change agent, therefore, is to balance the disconfirmation and the creation of anxiety.
- *Change*: Once a person or group is open to change there is an opportunity for the change agent to provide new information or perspectives on the topic under consideration. This happens because there is a relationship established and the individual or group has positively identified or connected with the change agent. Trust and relationship create a safe container

within which to do the work. Without safety, employees will not be able to access or use their creative energies.

- *Re-freezing*: Schein believed that the change needed to be congruent with the expectations and culture of the organization. The change must work within the work environment or the change will fail to take hold or maintain itself.

Ron Lippitt: Ronald Lippitt worked directly with Kurt Lewin and felt that his three stages of change needed to be expanded to five and that the term *phases* better described what actually occurred in the change process. Lippitt's phases are:

1. Development of the need for change.
2. Establishment of a change relationship between the change agent and the client organization.
3. Working toward change.
4. Generalization and stabilization of change.
5. Achieving a termination or ending the change contract between the consultant or change agent and the client organization.

Lippitt's work acknowledges the importance of the change agent role and clearly identifies a beginning and end to the event.

Peter Senge: In Chapter 2, I mentioned how we are using the U model created by Peter Senge, Otto Sharmer, and Betty Sue Flowers. Here, again, are the elements of the U model:

Sensing (Suspending): Gathering and considering information and mental models about the current state.

Redirecting: See things from a systemic and holistic way. Become aware that we may need to think about things differently and modify their current work activities.

Letting Go: Letting go of definitions of success and mental models that no longer serve our goals. Opening up our minds to new possibilities. Being more coachable.

Letting Come: This is the creative work that comes as much from the heart as well as the head. Having confidence in the rightness of right things. The essence or seed of the solution becomes conscious.

Crystallizing: Bringing together the new ideas to build a path forward.

Trying Out (Prototyping): Experimenting with new approaches. Learning from the process of trying. This step involves iterations— making adjustments based on the learning derived from trying it out.

Locking In (Institutionalizing): Adopting and forming new habits and regimens. The new becomes your natural.

We use the U model to ensure that we build self-awareness and strength on an individual basis and this helps us create the safe container that Schein articulated.

Peter Block: Peter Block, a writer, community activist, and organizational development thought leader, has contributed significantly to the literature about change management. His work has helped those in internal or external consulting roles understand and consider what's going on at each stage of the change process. At the very highest level his consulting model is comprised of four stages:

1. Contracting: Actions at this stage include developing a deep understanding of the problem, a clear expression of wants, an exploration of concerns about control and vulnerability, and giving support.
2. Diagnosis/Discovery: At this stage, Block suggests that consultants help employees treat each interaction as a learning event, identify current actions that contribute to the problem, and explore and clarify today's reality without judging it.
3. Feedback: During the third stage of change, it is important to funnel the data, present personal and organizational data, seek and manage feedback, focus on the current state, and help individuals' combat feelings of defensiveness.
4. Implementation: The final stage of change implementation should be characterized by high intensity participation, placing a variety of

choices on the table, changing the nature of conversations, transparency and the public expression of doubt, and co-creating structures to fit your purpose.

Here is one of my favorite quotes of Peter Block from his book, *Flawless Consulting*:

> Part of our task as consultants is to bring the right of assembly and freedom of speech into our organizations. In practical terms this means creating assemblies where there is an opportunity for all voices and points of view to be heard. Where reality in the words of the audience becomes as important as the reality spoken from the podium—perhaps more important. And where those at the podium tell the truth about failure and uncertainty.

William Bridges: The Bridges' model of transition distinguishes between changes and transitions. Bridges defines change as an external shift— something that happens. Examples include a new boss, work process changes, new coworker, merger, or acquisition. A transition is the psychological experience or reorientation process that precedes and accompanies the event. Transition is the process people go through when faced with a change. The Bridges' transition model focuses on how people transition and has three phases including:

- *Ending*: Before you can begin something new you must experience an end to the current state. The ending may require a letting go of old behaviors, beliefs, or self-perceptions. The ending results in loss, even when the change is perceived as favorable. The emotional response of ending may look like anger, bargaining, anxiety, sadness, or disorientation. To help people end and proceed through their transition, facilitators, leaders, and team members need to help mark the ending, define what's over and what's not, and treat the past with respect. When people get stuck in the ending phase, they resist change and revert to their old practices.

- *Neutral Zone*: Bridges described the neutral zone as the in-between state. It can be confusing, ambiguous, and uncomfortable. People feel like they are unsure what to do and where they fit in and this might lead them to feel anxious, overloaded, or overwhelmed. The neutral zone is also a very creative time because systems and processes are ripe for reinvention (correlates back to Lewin's unfreezing stage). Transition strategies for the neutral zone include defining what's known, creating temporary systems, strengthening connections between people and functions, engaging people in re-creating a new future, and increasing the frequency and openness of your communication.

- *New Beginning*: When the new change takes hold, people can shift into their new role and build routines. When we transition to the new beginning stage, we have accepted and adjusted to the change and our focus, comfort, and energy increases and stabilizes. Training, involvement, and communication are key actions that help bring the team's transition to the new beginning.

The inspiration we have derived from the Bridges model is most apparent in our team and individual phases of the Co-Create model.

Dr. John Kotter: Dr. John Kotter, professor emeritus at Harvard Business School, is well known for his contribution to the science of change management. In 1995, Kotter introduced his eight-step change process in his book, *Leading Change* and then drilled down on a portion of the model in *A Sense of Urgency*. Kotter observed that over 70 percent of all major change efforts in organizations fail. Our projects have the potential to add value to the business or fritter away its resources. Kotter's change process includes the following steps:

- Step One—Create Urgency: For change to happen, it helps if the whole company really wants it. Kotter urges us to develop a sense of urgency around the need for change.

- Step Two—Form a Powerful Coalition: It is critical to convince people that change is necessary. The initial phases of the Co-Create model are designed to create urgency and form a powerful coalition for change.
- Step Three—Create a Vision for Change: Kotter believed that ideas needed to be grounded by an overall vision. Our Co-Create defining stage help serve this need.
- Step Four—Communicate the Vision: What you do with your vision after you create it will determine your success. The commitment we make to ensure projects are inclusive and participatory processes helps us keep team members and stakeholders connected to the project.
- Step Five—Remove Obstacles: Kotter stressed the importance of removing sources of resistance or project failure and empowering people to execute the vision of the project.
- Step Six—Create Short-term Wins: Nothing motivates performance more than success, especially team success.
- Step Seven—Build on the Change: Kotter argues that many change projects fail because teams and leaders don't stick things through to the end. Quick wins are important but are not the same as victory.
- Step Eight—Anchor the Changes in Corporate Culture: Finally, to make any change stick, it should become part of our regular ways of working and culture.

Kotter felt that the toughest of the eight steps is creating a sense of urgency. This is particularly likely when too many number one priorities compete for our time and energy. We use our project roadmap and the Co-Create model to help ensure that we work on a project completely and well. We want to enable our employees to do their best work, not just more work.

David Herold and Donald Fedor: We love *Change the Way You Lead Change*, a book by Herold and Fedors because of the useful way they suggest that people think about and describe opportunities for change.

We particularly love their list of questions, organized into the following five sections:

1. What do you think needs changing?
2. Who should lead the change?
3. Who is expected to adopt the change?
4. What is the internal context like?
5. What is the external context like?

Our project owners refer to the complete list of questions when preparing their project whitepapers.

The Co-Create model is our framework for project management excellence and is a change model at its core. But as William Bridges acknowledged, it is the people who make change happen and who drive performance. Here are two experts in the fields of teaming that we were inspired by.

Peter Scholtes: Peter Scholtes' book, *The Team Handbook* is a classic and we refer to it often when preparing project whitepapers. Scholtes stresses the importance of thinking through not just what tasks need to be completed, but also how the work fits in with current processes, workloads, and the culture. Here are a few of my favorite questions from *The Team Handbook*:

- What is important to the customers about the product, process, or service?
- Why should the project or work be done now?
- How will the team focus its work?
- What business constraints must be taken into account in scheduling the project or work?
- Who can the team turn to for expert guidance and coaching for improvement?

As you have read throughout this book, we believe that the time you spend defining the current state and possibilities up front saves you time in the end and creates a better end product.

Bruce Tuckman: In Chapter 2, I shared Dr. Bruce Tuckman's model of team development. This model is an important reference point for how we ensure and improve the health of our team dynamics. Here, again, is a brief synopsis of the five stages of Tuckman model:

1. Forming: The initial stage of team development where members are getting oriented to one another and seeking to understand their roles and boundaries.
2. Storming: This stage of team development is characterized by style clashes, conflict, and working points of differentiation out. We find that familiar team members can go back to this phase when a new project or task brings disagreements to the surface.
3. Norming: The team is getting to know each other and is working through how to work well together. Their efforts look and feel more cohesive.
4. Performing: The team is utilizing the strengths of their relationships to get more done. Their ability to collaborate and solve problems is a competitive edge. Roles are flexible but clear.
5. Adjourning: The team creates closure for their work and feels complete in the task of marking the project's end.

Our teams talk about these stages and have learned these terms to help them self-diagnose teaming challenges and work through the stages of development together. And they know that any change—such as the introduction of new members or project setbacks—can cause the team to revert back to less developed stages.

ADDENDUM D

Team Output Examples

Are you ready to give the Co-Create model a try in your organization? Here are a few more examples you can refer to as you go through the phases of the model. I have changed the names of people involved and left out a few proprietary details, but have otherwise left the examples unchanged.

Phase 1—Whitepaper

Merchandising Structure Project

Purpose

To create a merchandising department structure that will lead customers at an increasing rate to perceive Hubert's assortment as unique and highly valued. This assortment will contribute to improving Hubert's strategic differentiation and result in faster sales and profit growth.

Situation Summary

The structure of the merchandising department has been re-evaluated twice in the last seven years. It was first reviewed in 2001, nearly seven years ago, when purchasing was separated from the department. This change allowed merchandising to become more product-focused and concentrate on the developmental aspect of the job. It was again reviewed in 2004, when the analysts were moved to marketing information services department (MKIS), further removing the transactional tasks from the developmental side of the business. Since that time, factors within the world, the foodservice market, and internal Hubert have changed considerably causing modifications in job responsibilities of each role. As business continues to get more complex it is necessary to regularly evaluate the model in order to meet the changing demands of the environment and remain competitive in the market.

Hubert's product development process has evolved significantly over the past three years. In the past Hubert was strictly a distributor and was not involved in decisions typically made by manufacturers. Merchandisers relied on manufacturers for most product development work and specification. With the growth of importing and the opportunity to have products manufactured exclusively for Hubert, merchandisers are now sourcing more like manufacturers. They are forced to not only pick winning products but creating product specifications and managing quality earlier in the developmental cycle. These tasks take more time and require new expertise for merchandising and the company.

Concurrent with these developments content management system (CMS) activities have become a larger percentage of the product manager's position. The result is this position has become more transactional. Merchandising has always had transactional activities, but many have moved in the last five years to other departments. CMS is the one transactional task that has expanded in this timeframe. If past experience is an indication it appears activity supporting CMS would be more productive if it were managed centrally. Today it is de-centralized overseen by individual merchandise managers.

This change in product manager responsibilities has caused a succession planning problem. Developmental tasks supporting product development and management have been de-emphasized. Proficiency in transactional work has been valued. The result is the product manager position is manned by individuals who are practicing skills that are not preparing them for the next position, merchandise manager. That position is primarily strategic and developmental.

At this point it does not appear the existing product managers have the skills, and aptitude for the merchandise manager position.

Four of Hubert's five merchandisers are the original group that came to the company when the department was formed. Their contribution has been a key driver of Hubert's success the last 20 years. Throughout their careers they have acquired valuable knowledge and expertise regarding markets, competitors, vendors, importing procedures, and product knowledge. This expertise has proven to be critical in developing the product assortment.

One, or more, of the merchandise managers are within five years of possible retirement. It is imperative Hubert has employees identified and trained to potentially take over for these individuals.

Looking into the future of Hubert, merchandising must be positioned to continue to add value to Hubert by increasing the uniqueness and value of Hubert's assortment. The number of pages and products a merchandiser will be expected to manage is projected to increase substantially over the next three years. In 2008, there will be 48 pages added to the Source Book, GR Retail Resource, and German Book during the same catalog drop. This trend is expected to continue over the following two years, adding more pages each year. The second brand may also impact the workload of the department.

Given the changes in the market, manufacturing environment, lack of individuals ready to step into the merchandiser position, and projected workload in the next three years we need to review the structure and better prepare the department for the future.

Scope

This project will focus on the structure in the merchandising department and will consider and realign roles and responsibilities based on what we know about current and future expectations for department contributions to the business. The team will complete and implement a recruitment strategy and plan and personnel training materials for any new positions developed.

Process

AH will be the project sponsor. The project will focus on defining and planning the merchandising department reorganization, as it functions today. A team will be assembled that will include AH, PC, LVS, DL, CM, and GH. Steve Martin will facilitate the meetings. Others may be asked to participate when specific issues need to be addressed.

The team will meet once a week beginning January 2008. The plan for new roles and responsibilities will be identified by April 1. Recruiting process to take place April—September. The new structure will be in place by December 1, 2008.

Issues to Be Addressed

1. Review and confirm the organizational objectives, skill sets and structure proposed by PC and AH. Incorporate feedback from group into proposal.
2. Review the present roles and responsibilities of the existing positions. Which tasks are transactional and which are strategic?
3. Create responsibilities and accountabilities for new positions created in the department.
4. Create skill sets, attributes and experience needed for the hiring of these new positions.
5. How do we create an environment to attract, train, and develop potential individuals for the merchandise manager position?
6. Plan for hiring four new individuals within six months.
7. What processes will be impacted by this organizational change? What process changes will have to be made?
8. Potential for new management position? What skill sets will be required for this position?
9. How should the current positions change?
10. Focus on product strategy and development?
11. Develop communication to department notifying them of organizational changes.
12. Consider current personnel and how they will fit into the revised department structure.
13. Work with performance management system in developing compensation and recruiting strategy.
14. Develop effective process for training new personnel.

Outcome

The final outcome of this project will be an aligned department organizational structure that will position merchandising for the future. As a part of this project, the team will flesh out and define any new position descriptions, roles, and responsibilities, and key processes needed to support the strategy and new positions. The new department structure should be fully operational by December 1, 2008.

Phase 1—Team Development—Forming Example

Rules for engagement

- Balance confidentiality and communication.
- Ask the team about what to communicate outside the meetings.
- It's ok to restate the business case to others in the department.
- We want to be open to new task/responsibility assignments that surface.
- We need every team member to provide his or her opinion.
- We will respect each other's opinions.

Phase 2—Discovery Checklist of Tasks Completed

- Gathered and reviewed all the current merchandise manager performance management documents to identify responsibilities and tasks.
- Gathered and reviewed all the current product manager performance management documents to identify responsibilities and tasks.
- Reviewed the current process/workflow information to further determine who was doing what.
- Categorized all tasks and responsibilities as either transactional or strategic (creative).

Phase 3—Co-Create Example

Merchandising Re-Organization Project
New Position Descriptions—Input
February 7, 2008

Merchandise Manager

Responsibilities/Tasks

1. Assortment management
   - Provide strategic direction to category manager
   - Provide information regarding market, vendors, and so on
   - Accountable for final decisions.
2. New product development

Category Manager

Responsibilities/Tasks

1. Assortment management
   - Primary focus on existing, domestic vendors
   - Provide analysis and recommendations to MM for all DCS merchandise managers and all category levels.
2. Product development
   - Follow up on MM international sourcing trips
     - Manage and follow through on the details
     - Complete import profitability analysis.

Transactional Position (title TBD)

Responsibilities/Tasks

1. Manage and execute CMS presentation process for all catalogs
   - Comply with all standard CMS processes
   - Create presentations and populate appropriate data fields
   - Enter product specs and features, advantages and benefits FABs for copy
   - Follow up on samples or JPEG images for photography
   - Proof all presentations for accuracy following established guidelines and meet all CMS deadlines.
2. CMS maintenance
   - Enter all vendor initiated changes—dropped items, changes to specs, photo, and so on.

3. T500 maintenance
  • Ex. catalog corrections, collection codes.

End of Phase 3 and beginning of Phase 4 Example—this is the content from a PowerPoint Presentation from a meeting with all the stakeholders.

Merchandising Department Restructure

Agenda

  • Review of white paper—PC
  • Continual Process Improvement method (CPI)—PC
  • Introduce new structure—PC
  • Department Positions—PC CM, DL
  • Hiring and interview process—LVS
  • Implementation going forward—PC
  • Questions

Review White Paper

  • Purpose
    o To develop a personnel structure within the merchandising department that will allow Hubert to create a unique assortment that accelerates our growth rate.
  • Objectives
    o Increase productivity by consolidating transactional activity
    o Develop competency in overseas sourcing
    o Make succession planning possible
    o Continue to lead industry in innovation and creativity.
  • Product development process
    o Past—merchandisers chose existing product
    o Current—merchandisers involved in developing new product
    o Future—merchandisers specifying product and searching for qualified manufacturer.

- CMS
  - o Still requires merchandisers to manage transactional requirements of business
  - o Not their competency.
- Succession planning
  - o Merchandise manager is key position in company
  - o Important to have individuals trained to step into position.
- Issues addressed
  - o Review current roles and responsibilities
  - o Transactional or strategic
  - o Environment to attract, train, develop
  - o Merchandiser position change to focus on product strategy and development
  - o Identify skills required to develop and source products.

CPI Process

- Committee members
  - o AH—sponsor
  - o Steve Martin—facilitator
  - o Members: PC, LVS, GH, CM, DL.
- Identified all tasks for merchandising
- Divided them into appropriate categories
  - o Strategic or transactional.
- Separate tasks by function
- Wrote roles and responsibilities for each function
- Assembled structure and number of individuals in each role
- Submitted proposal for approval from Bart and TAKKT Board
- Still to complete
  - o Process work for new responsibilities
  - o Fill open positions
  - o Training.

Introduce New Structure

- Realignment of positions and people
- Have more jobs than people

- Everyone will have a job in the new structure
- Posting new positions this afternoon
- Pay ranges
  - Category manager
  - Marketing content specialist.

Department Positions

- Merchandise manager
  - Assortment management and pricing
  - Product development
  - Travel and sourcing
  - Special projects
  - Business development
  - Web merchandising
  - Product knowledge and training
  - Staff development.
- Marketing content manager
  - Manage and execute CMS presentation process for all catalogs, print, web
  - CMS maintenance
  - Manage and execute T500 process
  - Training of T500 and CMS
  - Endeca input
  - Merchandising Pindar expert
  - Manage and develop staff.
- Category manager
  - Assortment management
  - Product development
  - Pricing
  - Product training
  - Sales support
  - Special projects
  - Developmental projects
  - Requirements and attributes.
- Marketing content specialist
  - Manage and execute CMS process for all catalogs, print, web

- o CMS maintenance
- o Manage and execute T500 process
- o Assist with product training
- o Endeca input
- o Requirements and attributes.

Hiring and Interview Process

- • Timeline
  - o By June 1st—post opening for category manager and content specialist internally, advertise externally for category manager
  - o By September 1st—all positions filled and training begins
  - o By December 1st—new structure is fully operational.
- • Current product managers
  - o Need to complete job interest form for desired position
    - ▪ Category manager
    - ▪ Marketing content specialist.
- • By July 15th
- • Decisions for internal candidates—interviews
- • Category manager
  - o Interview—PC, MW, and LH
  - o Assessment—Chally, Excel for external candidates only
  - o Final Interview—candidate will be interviewed by two merchandise managers and Andy. Presentation for external candidates only
  - o Interviews—external candidates only
- • Marketing content specialist
  - o Interview—PC, JM, and LH
  - o Assessment—Chally, KS will provide assessment of technical skills
  - o Final interview—if necessary.

Going Forward

- • New processes to develop
  - o Will be determined during the same time as interview process

- o Communication within department
- o Who is responsible for specific tasks.
- • Transition period

Phase 3 Co-Create the Ideal Examples

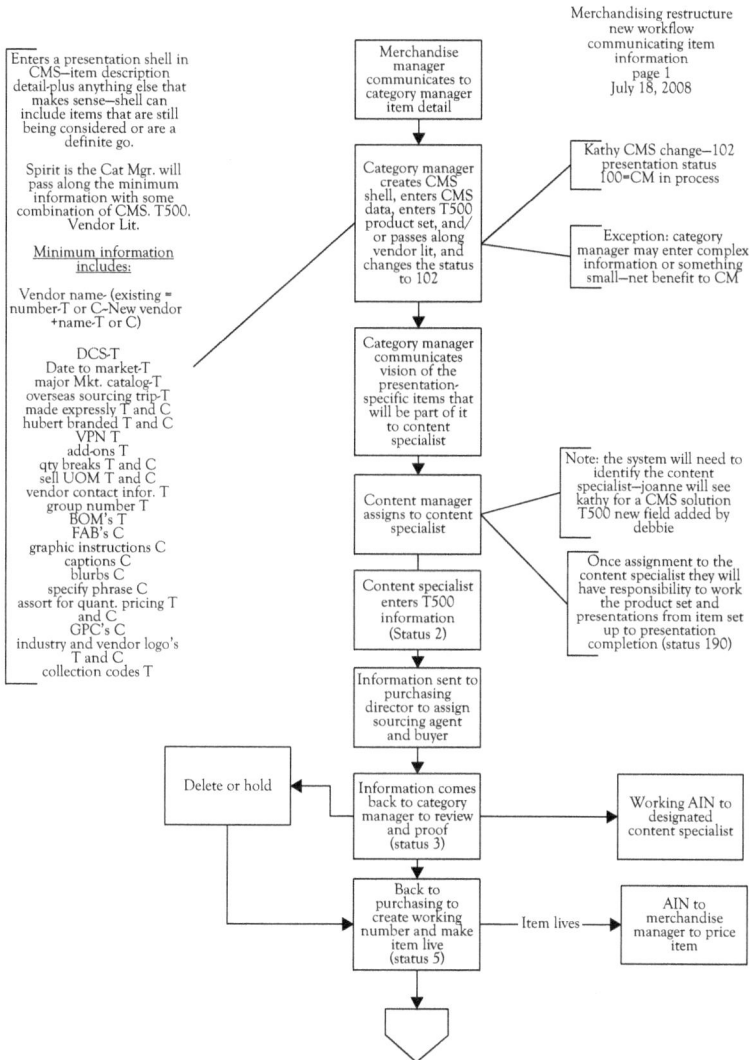

Merchandising restructure
new workflow
communicating item
information
page 1
July 18, 2008

```
┌─────────────────────┐        ┌──────────────────┐
│ Enters a presentation│        │   Merchandise    │
│ shell in CMS—item   │        │    manager       │
│ description detail-  │        │ communicates to  │
│ plus anything else   │        │ category manager │
│ that makes sense—    │        │   item detail    │
│ shell can include    │        └──────────────────┘
│ items that are still │                 │
│ being considered or  │                 ▼
│ are a definite go.   │        ┌──────────────────┐    Kathy CMS change—102
│                      │        │ Category manager │    presentation status
│ Spirit is the Cat    │        │   creates CMS    │    100=CM in process
│ Mgr. will pass along │        │ shell, enters CMS│
│ the minimum          │        │ data, enters T500│
│ information with some │        │ product set, and/│    Exception: category
│ combination of CMS.  │        │ or passes along  │    manager may enter complex
│ T500. Vendor Lit.    │        │ vendor lit, and  │    information or something
│                      │        │ changes the      │    small—net benefit to CM
│ Minimum information  │        │ status to 102    │
│ includes:            │        └──────────────────┘
│                      │                 │
│ Vendor name- (existing│                ▼
│ = number-T or C-New  │        ┌──────────────────┐
│ vendor +name-T or C) │        │ Category manager │
│                      │        │ communicates     │
│         DCS-T        │        │ vision of the    │
│ Date to market-T     │        │ presentation-    │
│ major Mkt. catalog-T │        │ specific items   │
│ overseas sourcing    │        │ that will be     │
│ trip-T               │        │ part of it to    │
│ made expressly T and │        │ content          │
│ C                    │        │ specialist       │
│ hubert branded T and │        └──────────────────┘
│ C                    │                 │         Note: the system will need to
│         VPN T        │                 ▼         identify the content
│      add-ons T       │        ┌──────────────────┐ specialist—joanne will see
│ qty breaks T and C   │        │ Content manager  │ kathy for a CMS solution
│ sell UOM T and C     │        │ assigns to       │ T500 new field added by
│ vendor contact infor.│        │ content          │ debbie
│ T                    │        │ specialist       │
│ group number T       │        └──────────────────┘  Once assignment to the
│       BOM's T        │                 │          content specialist they will
│       FAB's C        │                 ▼          have responsibility to work
│ graphic instructions │        ┌──────────────────┐ the product set and
│ C                    │        │ Content specialist│ presentations from item set
│     captions C       │        │ enters T500      │ up to presentation
│      blurbs C        │        │ information      │ completion (status 190)
│ specify phrase C     │        │   (Status 2)     │
│ assort for quant.    │        └──────────────────┘
│ pricing T and C      │                 │
│       GPC's C        │                 ▼
│ industry and vendor  │        ┌──────────────────┐
│ logo's T and C       │        │ Information sent  │
│ collection codes T   │        │ to purchasing    │
└─────────────────────┘        │ director to      │
                                │ assign sourcing  │
                                │ agent and buyer  │
                                └──────────────────┘
                                         │
        ┌──────────────┐        ┌──────────────────┐        ┌──────────────┐
        │Delete or hold│◄───────│ Information comes │───────►│ Working AIN  │
        └──────────────┘        │ back to category │        │ to designated│
                                │ manager to review│        │ content      │
                                │ and proof        │        │ specialist   │
                                │  (status 3)      │        └──────────────┘
                                └──────────────────┘
                                         │
                                ┌──────────────────┐        ┌──────────────┐
                                │ Back to          │        │  AIN to      │
                                │ purchasing to    │        │ merchandise  │
                                │ create working   │─Item──►│ manager to   │
                                │ number and make  │ lives  │ price item   │
                                │ item live        │        └──────────────┘
                                │  (status 5)      │
                                └──────────────────┘
                                         │
                                         ▼
```

Merchandising restructure
new workflow
communicating item
information
page 2
July 18, 2008

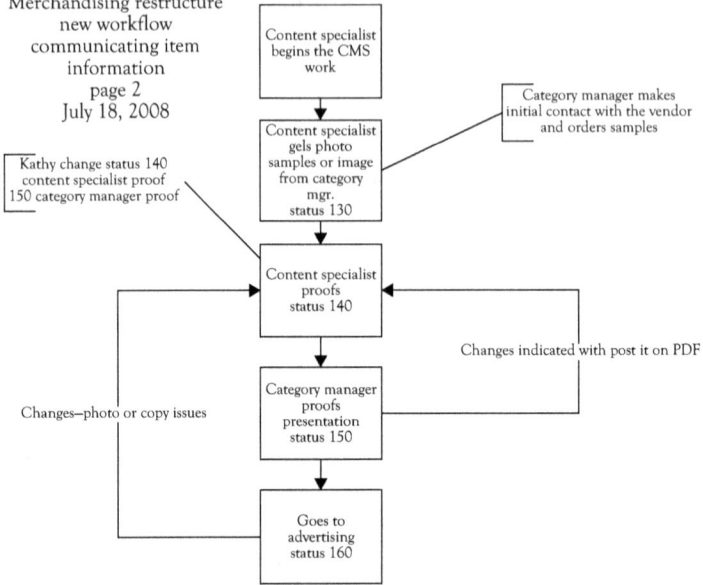

Content specialist
begins the CMS
work

Category manager makes
initial contact with the vendor
and orders samples

Content specialist
gels photo
samples or image
from category
mgr.
status 130

Kathy change status 140
content specialist proof
150 category manager proof

Content specialist
proofs
status 140

Changes indicated with post it on PDF

Category manager
proofs
presentation
status 150

Changes—photo or copy issues

Goes to
advertising
status 160

Merchandising restructure
new workflow
T500 maintenance
July 1, 2008

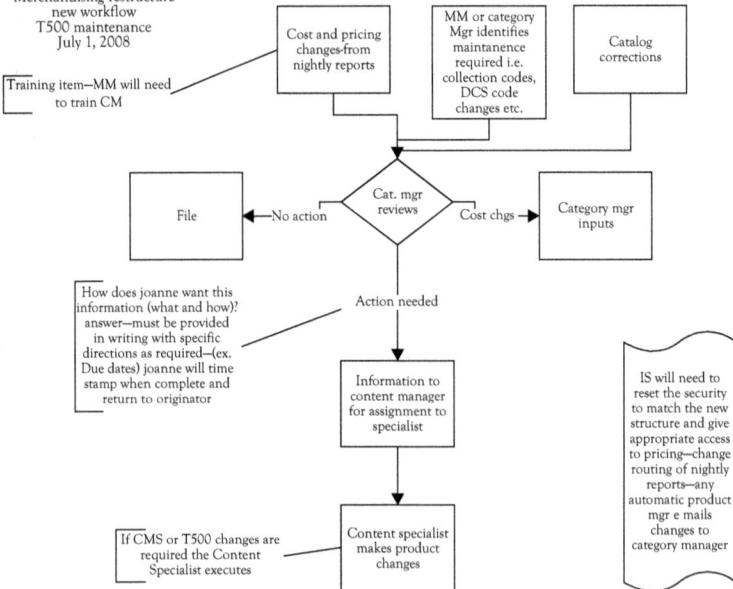

Cost and pricing
changes-from
nightly reports

MM or category
Mgr identifies
maintenance
required i.e.
collection codes,
DCS code
changes etc.

Catalog
corrections

Training item—MM will need
to train CM

Cat. mgr
reviews

File   ◄—No action

Cost chgs►   Category mgr
inputs

How does joanne want this
information (what and how)?
answer—must be provided
in writing with specific
directions as required—(ex.
Due dates) joanne will time
stamp when complete and
return to originator

Action needed

Information to
content manager
for assignment to
specialist

IS will need to
reset the security
to match the new
structure and give
appropriate access
to pricing—change
routing of nightly
reports—any
automatic product
mgr e mails
changes to
category manager

If CMS or T500 changes are
required the Content
Specialist executes

Content specialist
makes product
changes

Phase 1—Defining Example—Nonstock White Paper

Revised 2-1-08

Purpose

Develop a streamlined process to enhance the customer experience by improving response time and providing visibility for this category of business.

Situation Summary

Nonstocks originate from customer requests for products not carried in Hubert's current assortment. Nonstocks are a value-added service that, when done well, provide a competitive advantage for the company. It is believed that providing this service enhances customer relationships and generates additional business.

Requests range from a different color of an item we currently carry, to requests for customized products and occasionally for product lines that Hubert does not carry, for example cash registers and flooring material. Requests can be for replacement parts, forwarded from the sourcing agent to a buyer to complete, a request for a one-time purchase of an item that becomes an SO.#, or an ongoing purchase for a customer program, which becomes a five-digit "S" item. Owing to the wide scope of products that are requested, getting complete information is a challenge and creates additional communication between purchasing, the vendor, sales, and the customer.

Guidelines have been established to address qualifications required when initiating the nonstock request. The guidelines and requirements have created confusion regarding reorders, discontinued products, assigned versus unassigned accounts, required GP, minimum cost, and so on. In 2006, 5 percent of the nonstocks received did not meet the required guidelines.

Nonstocks are submitted in Outlook via e-mail, generated by Account Services Reps, Account Development ManagersASRs, ADMs, and Inbound Call Center. There is no direct link between the information provided on the nonstock form and what is entered into the T500. If the item is converted to a five-digit "S," all the information that was provided on the nonstock has to be entered into the system. The buyer has to find the original information or contact the vendor again. This creates duplicate work that equals inefficiency. The tracking process is currently a cumbersome manual process and there is no way to capture which nonstocks are converted into actual orders.

Sourcing agents experience frustration due to the amount of nonstocks received, inadequate information provided, requests to add a new vendor for one item, and requests that do not meet the guidelines and requirements. There is also concern expressed regarding the prioritization of nonstocks versus cost negotiation, rebate collection, alternate sourcing, and building vendor relationships in order to increase the profitability of the company.

Sales experiences frustration due to a lack of understanding of vendor response time, and the amount of information needed to complete a nonstock. Response time from the sourcing agent for a nonassortment item that exists in a current vendor line is three business days. Customer perception is that it takes too long to get an answer, even though 61 percent of requests were returned within 24 hours, and an additional 14 percent within two to three days. Response for a "custom" item, or an item that has to be sourced from a supplier not currently a Hubert vendor is seven business days. Custom nonstocks involve additional customer "proofing" steps, and sometimes include coordinating artwork design. Currently all nonstocks are completed by the three sourcing agents. Requests for replacement parts are forwarded onto the buyers. The volume of nonstocks initiated, the time frames established for response time, and customer expectations creates frustration for both sales and purchasing.

Direct contact between sales and customers with the vendors can occur if more detailed information is needed when working on custom quotes. It is necessary for the sourcing agent to initiate the contact, document any changes made to the original request, and maintain art and proof approval until project completion. In some instances calls are made to vendors without purchasing involvement. The result is confusion relating to price, lead times, minimum required quantity purchases, discounts, and proof approval.

Recap of Nonstocks

All nonstocks received in 2006 were reviewed in order to compile data by top three, top 20, and "All Other" customers. "All Other" may include top three and top 20 accounts if the name on the nonstock did not clearly identify that customer as fitting in to one of those groups. This detailed information was compiled manually and is not available for previous years. Some nonstocks have more than one item per from which accounts for the discrepancy between new items set up and nonstocks received.

2006 Nonstock Sourcing

2006 Nonstock recap	Total	Top xxx	Top xxx	All other
Nonstocks received	3,389	955	570	1,864
% of Nonstocks		28%	17%	55%
Total new items set up	4,753			
SO.#	4,171			
5 digit "S"	582			
Items with sales	2,112			
Items with no activity	2,641			

There were 892 received out of the total classified as "No Quotes." These are nonstocks received that did not meet the guidelines (187) or having no source available (577) and returned to sales for clarification and not received back (128). The "No Quotes" account for 26 percent of total nonstocks received. Over half, 56 percent of new "S" and SO# items set up had no sales activity.

Total Company Sales GP% vs. S/SO Sales GP%

	2006 sales	%	Margin	GP	%
Total co.	$xxx		xxx%	$xxx	
S & SO	$xxx	xxx%	xxx%	$xxx	xxx%

	2005 sales	%	Margin	GP	%
Total co.	$xxx		xxx%	$xxx	
S & SO	$xxx	xxx%	xxx%	$xxx	xxx%

	2004 sales	%	Margin	GP	%
Total co.	$xxx		xxx%	$xxx	
S & SO	$xxx	xxx%	xxx%	$xxx	xxx%

Cost Benefit—2006 S and SO# Sales and Profitability

	2006 sales $	% of total	2006 GP $	% of total	2006 ABC costing
Set up in 2006 S & SO	$xxx	xxx%	$xxx	xxx%	
Set up prior to 2006 S & SO	$xxx	xxx%	$xxx	xxx%	
Total	**$xxx**	xxx%	**$xxx**	xxx%	**$xxx**

The total cost, $xxx, based on SO cost object, included sales and warehouse costs and accounted for 21,000 lines. The purchasing department's portion of the total ABC costing in 2006 for nonstocks was $xxx. Sales cost for the same period was $xxx. S/SO business profitability is $xxx.

Objectives

Implement one process/program where nonstock requests are submitted, SO.#'s are entered and converted, conversion rate is tracked, and sales and GP dollars are available to measure the profitability of nonstocks as a value-added service.

1. Develop integrated software solution.
2. Develop criteria for nonstocks going forward.
3. Determine competitive response time goals, establish benchmark criteria.
4. Determine the structure to support the procedure.
5. Determine where responsibility belongs and the amount of staffing needed to achieve response time goal.
6. Define compensation, adjust performance review system.
7. Develop guidelines for direct sales contact with vendor.
8. Re-evaluate margin (expectation from current guidelines xx%).
9. Evaluate liquidations.

Process

A cross-functional team will be selected to complete this project. Team members from purchasing will include TB, MM, and JH. Representatives from sales will be CK, KS, MEG, and ST. DS will join us from information systems. As specific issues surface, other departments (i.e., merchandising) may be asked to participate.

The CPI process will be facilitated by Steve Martin. MR and DT are the project sponsors.

Outcome

Increase the response rate of nonstocks returned within 24 hours.

Decrease ABC cost per nonstock by reducing duplicate steps now required by sales and purchasing. A higher conversion rate based on quicker response time would result in increased sales.

Phase 3—Co-Create the Ideal Example

Working title—nonstock specialist responsibilities

1. Develop customer relationships—identify and clarify the customers nonstock order needs.
   Possible performance measures:
   - Use of LAER
   - Percent meeting Hubert nonstock guidelines
   - Percent returned
   - Productivity—calls taken, nonstocks worked
   - Conversion rate
2. Market and product knowledge—attain an expert level
3. Possible performance measures:
   - Attendance at product training
   - Attending trade shows
   - Vendor site visits
   - Use of internal software or people resources
4. Customer service—meet or exceed service commitments
   Possible performance measures:

- Nonstock cycle time
- Order cycle time—contact customer with status if it changes
- Accuracy of entered orders
- Response time
- Percent first call resolution

5. Develop and maintain positive vendor relationships.

   Possible performance measures:
   - Professional interaction (observations/monitoring calls)
   - Setting clear service expectations
   - Vendor selection—utilizes vendors per Hubert Guidelines

6. Maintains and analyzes system information

   Possible performance measures:
   - Accuracy
   - Completeness
   - Timeliness

7. Manage nonstock profitability—meet or exceed profitability goals— includes cost and customer pricing

   Possible performance measures:
   - Conversion rate
   - ABC Activity Based Costing measure?
   - Other measures TBD

8. Meets cultural expectations

Dimensions: (Note—We Need to Do a Priority Matrix)

- Decision making
- Adaptability
- Negotiation
- Managing work
- Continuous learning
- Customer focus
- Building strategic working relationships
- Stress tolerance
- Follow up
- Initiating action

Requirements

- Excel
- Experience working with food service equipment and supplies
- Four-year college degree or equivalent experience
- Strong written and verbal communication skills

Desirables

- Experience with auto quotes or similar system
- T500 experience
- Experience sourcing food service equipment and supplies
- Previous customer service experience

Lead nonstock specialist—includes the above responsibilities, dimensions, requirements, and desirables plus...

Responsibilities

- Supervise, train, and mentor staff. This includes generating and participating in the review process and performance coaching. It does not include hiring, firing, or determining compensation.
- Process management. This includes tracking standards.
- Special projects

Dimensions

- Coaching
- Building trust

Staffing Recommendation—Outline

- Four nonstock specialists (3 January start-up—1 in July)
- One lead (working)
- Rationale

- Current three sourcing agents are spending 80 percent of their time working nonstocks.
- Response to the customer satisfaction results.
- Available to talk to customers as they call—reduce the nonproductive nonstocks in the system.
- Sourcing agents able to do their job in working to reduce the cost of goods of current assortment.
- Improved customer experience by…
  - Increasing first contact resolution
  - Quicker response time
  - Creating one point of contact
  - Connecting with product experts
  - Creating internal accountability.
- This gives us the ability to market and sell this service— will create a scalable model

Phase 4—Implementation Planning Example

Formal Request for Nonstock Department Resources

Background

In early 2008, a cross-functional group formed a CPI team to develop a streamlined process to enhance the customer experience related to sourcing of nonassortment products. The need was exposed during the TAKKT customer survey in 2006 as a revenue opportunity that fell within the hidden opportunity quadrant for customer retention for top 20 and new customers. This will be achieved through improving response time and providing visibility for this category of business.

Process

Cross-functional team members were assembled to take on the task of discovering the best process to achieve these goals. Purchasing representation included TB, MM and JH. KS, CK, MEG and ST provide the representation for sales, rounded out by DS from IS and Steve

Martin as the project facilitator. The nine objectives of this project were as follows:

1. Develop an integrated software solution.
2. Develop criteria for nonstocks going forward.
3. Provide competitive response time goals through benchmarking.
4. Determine the structure to support the procedure.
5. Determine where responsibility belongs and the amount of staffing needed to achieve response time goals.
6. Define compensation and adjust the review system for this position.
7. Develop guidelines for direct sales contact with the vendor.
8. Re-evaluate margin (expectation from current guidelines is xx%).
9. Evaluate liquidations.

Discovery

Through comprehensive analysis of the current nonassortment sourcing processes, it was apparent that we are not currently meeting the needs of both internal and external customers. It was also recognized that our three sourcing agents were spending 80 percent of their time working nonassortment requests. Nonassortment products accounted for over $xxx in profitability for fiscal year 2006. A total of 3,389 nonstocks were requested by customers in 2006. Of these 45 percent were for our top 20 customers and the remaining were for all other customers. At the same time, about 50 percent of the total nonassortment products that were set up were ordered, a percentage that can be improved through timely conversion of requests to orders.

Response time was recognized as another shortcoming of the current process. Hubert currently has sourcing listed as one of the links on the value chain, yet a little less than 40 percent of our customer's requests take over 24 hours to resolve. We recognize that this process needs to be faster and a standard will be put into place based on benchmarking data that we are currently acquiring. Frustration also exists on an internal level due to incomplete information which requires rework, too many people involved in the process, and finally, a lack of transparency of the status of requests.

Recommendation

The group has come up with the following recommendation: The non-assortment sourcing function at Hubert needs to be confined to its own department and that functional responsibility needs to live within the customer services area of sales. The responsibilities of this position will include the development of customer relations, market and product knowledge, customer service, the development and maintenance of vendor relationships, maintenance, and analysis of system information, the management of nonassortment profitability and finally, adherence to cultural expectations. In addition, a lead will need to be in place to manage and mentor the front line staff, manage processes, and manage special projects. In addition, this will be a working lead, managing all other aspects of the job as the frontline position.

Some of the reasons that this position will report to sales are as follows. The nonstock position will have direct contact with the customer. This will allow many steps of the current process to be eliminated, since they will be speaking with the end user. As a customer facing position, this position will develop extensive customer knowledge in addition to the product knowledge that they offer, allowing us to manage profitability better than we are today. We will also be able to better manage how these processes impact the customer and react in a more timely and customer-centric way.

To handle this, we are requesting three frontline positions, starting in January 2009 along with a department lead. These positions will be managed as a separate department and report to GH. We would also like to have the option of adding an additional frontline position in July, based on the impact that we see in the first six months of this department. At that time, we would consider expanding the nonassortment program to customers outside of our assigned markets and reassess current guidelines to open up more revenue-generating opportunities for Hubert, as long as they meet our profitability objectives.

Outcome

- Improvement in response time, thus improving customer satisfaction, a negative area identified through the TAKKT customer survey. Studies show that there is a 20 percent drop in individual customer satisfaction for each additional contact that needs to be made to or from a company.

- Freeing up sourcing agents, who currently spend over 80 percent of their time with this function, to allow them to find alternative vendors and better cost opportunities for our core products.
- Elimination of nonproductive nonstocks (currently at 33 percent), because the end user will be speaking directly with the Hubert representative that has the task of finding the nonassortment product.
- The ability to market this service since we will have the resources in place to support it, truly making this a competency.
- Increased revenue opportunities as we expand the guidelines from our current limitations.

Training Plan with Execution Details—New SOS Department and Special Order Agents

17-Dec-08

Training topic	Learning objectives	How	Trainer/ Resource
Guidelines— sales and SOS	Gain an overall understanding of the guidelines including decision-making criteria—clear roles and responsibilities of each department. Additionally this will cover pricing, calculating GP profitability.	Guideline documents supported by training— broken down by functional areas—SOS, developers, ASR's remaining customer Op's, purchasing, merchandising— overview only— accounting, marketing, DC mgmt.	SOS department manager, ASR's— Sherri, developers— KS and CK customer Op's-ME, RR, CM., purchasing/ merchandising— JH MM, TB
Review old and new process	Review for understanding— emphasizing change of roles, benefits of new process, strategy implication—selling more stuff to existing customers.	Same as guidelines	Same as guidelines

Training topic	Learning objectives	How	Trainer/ Resource
New software	SOS—cover the mechanic's—how it works, security, linkage to the guidelines. All other departments will need to know how to search and enter a nonstock.	SOS—hands-on training with software using training scenario's —use PC Lab—can use the actual system and wipe out the training material. Inbound, ASR's, developers, purchasing departments will need hands-on training—tutorial being developed.	A person will be assigned in the SOS department—will be supported by Sri for the rollout. Ronda Russell will support the training design and other departments. Robb creating tutorial.
How to price for contract customers	Understand, in detail, customer-specific deals— as well as product segment pricing goals.	Documents will need to be developed describing the deals for SOS use. This should be organized in a standard way.	Developers and ASR's

Training topic	Time required	To do's
Guidelines—sales and SOS	SOS—One day, other departments covered in a two-hour meeting	1. Finish guidelines—GH, 2. Sign off with MR—complete, 3. Training materials developed by department—GH
Review old and new process	Covered in guideline meeting	
New software	SOS TBD, all other departments covered in the two-hour meeting outlined above.	
How to price for contract customers	Covered in guideline meeting— see above	KS and CK gathering the information and create a template for use across multiple customers—complete

Training topic	Learning objectives	How	Trainer/ Resource
Product knowledge	Generalist knowl-edge for all—expert knowledge for SOS agent specialty	Generalist knowledge will be gained, building on their current product knowledge, by attending vendor fairs, catalog cram, and regular	Merchandise and category managers

		product trainings. Expert knowledge will be gained by partnering with merchandising to do the regular product training and catalog crams, being involved on vendor meetings and visits, meetings with merchandise and category managers.	
Time management	TBD		
Sales T500	Order entry, order detail, and look up	Modified version of Customer Op Program	RR
Negotiating skills	Understand the stakeholder model and the interests of the various parties	Business tools training—ASR Program	RB
CSE	Establish customer interaction skills— train all the basic Carew models	Existing program for those who need it	RM
Autoquotes	Develop basic skills in using the software—use of catalog and setting up spreadsheets	Morning sessions—cover content—afternoon application exercises— training material available on Autoquote website	Special agent JH
Vendor visits	Develop relationships, understand capabilities, new products, current issues, and so on.	Will be involved when vendor visits Hubert—agents could go on visits to the vendor	Sourcing agents will notify, merchandise managers as well— coordinated with SOS manager

Training topic	Time required	To do's
Product knowledge	Ongoing	GH to meet with PC to see if she supports the ideas—complete. Greg will get additional input from the merchandise managers. Will get started after Cram

Training topic	Time required	To do's
Time management		
Sales T500	TBD	ME—talk to RR and figure out the modified version—complete
Negotiating skills	One hour	Schedule when ready
CSE		SM—get dates for GH—na
Autoquotes	Two days	JH—download the training materials —when ready set up a meeting with Steve to design program—complete
Vendor visits	?	GH—review with KK and PC— complete

Training topic	Time required	To do's
Vendor interaction— guidelines, pricing structures, order cycle times, lead-times	Two hours	GH—review with KK— complete
T500—item setup, assigning DCS codes, inquiries, vendor contacts, finding freight factors	Four hours	JH— review the existing training material and figure out a specific plan—complete
Vendor strategy/ knowledge— who does what—preferred vendors	TBD	
ACD phone training	One hour	

Bibliography

Bellah, R., R. Madsen, W. Sullivan, A. Swidler, and S. Tipton. 1985. *Habits of the Heart: Individualism and Commitment in American Life*. New York, NY: Harper & Row.

Block, P. 2012. *Flawless Consulting*. 3rd ed. San Francisco, CA; Jossey-Bass.

Block, P. 2002. *The Answer to How is Yes*. San Francisco, CA; Berrett- Koehler.

Bridges, W. 1991. *Managing Transitions*. 2nd ed. Cambridge MA; DaCapo Press.

Collins, J.C. 2001. *Good to Great*. New York, NY: HarperCollins.

Damon, W., J. Menon, and K.C. Bronk. 2003. "The Development of Purpose." *Applied Developmental Science* 7, no. 3, pp. 119–28, 121.

Dik, B., and R. Duffey. 2012. *Make Your Job a Calling*. Templton Press.

Dik, B., and R. Duffey. 2009. "Call and Vocation at Work: Definitions and Prospects for Research and Practice." *Counseling Psychologist* 37, no. 3, pp. 424–50, 427.

Herold, D., and D. Feders. 2008. *Change The Way You Lead Change: Leadership Strategies That Really Work*. Stanford, CA: Stanford University Press.

Katzenbach, J., and D. Smith. 1993. *The Wisdom of Teams*. Boston, MA: Harvard Business Review Press.

Kotter, J. 2008. *A Sense of Urgency*. Boston, MA: Harvard Business Press.

Kotter, J. 1996. *Leading Change*. Boston, MA: Harvard Business Press.

Lencioni, P. 2012. *The Advantage—Why Organizational Health Trumps Everything Else in Business*. Jossey-Bass.

Lewin, K. 1947. "Group Decision and Social Change." In *Readings in Social Psychology*, eds. T.M. Newcomb, E.L. Hartley et al. New York, NY: Henry Holt.

Lippitt, R., J. Watson, and B. Westley. 1958. *Dynamics of Planned Change*. New York, NY: Harcourt Brace.

Madonna, J. 1997. *Mission Possible*. In K. Blanchard and T. Waghorn. McGraw-Hill.

Project Management Institute. 2008. *A Guide to the Project Management Body of Knowledge*. Newton Square, PA: PMI.

Schein, E.H. 1987. *Process Consultation: Its role in Organization Development*. 2nd ed. 2 Vols. Reading MA: Addison-Wesley.

Scholtes, P.R., B.L. Joiner, and B.J. Streibel. 2003. *The Team Handbook*. 3rd ed. Madison, WI: Oriel.

Senge, P., C.O. Scharmer, J. Jaworski, and B.S. Flowers. 2005. *Presence: Human Purpose and the Field of the Future*. New York, NY: Crown Business.

Senge, P. 1990. *The Fifth Discipline*. Century Business.

Tuckman, B. 1965. "Developmental Sequence in Small Groups." *Psychological Bulletin*, American *Psychological Association* 63, no. 6, pp. 384–9.

Tuckman, B., and M. Jensen. 1977. "Stages of Small Group Development Revisited." *Group and Organizational Studies* 2, pp. 419–27.

Tuckman, B. 2011. *Citation Classic-Developmental Sequence in Small Groups, Current Concerns*. Retrieved on April 24 from www.garfield.library.upenn. edu/classics1984TD25600001.pdf

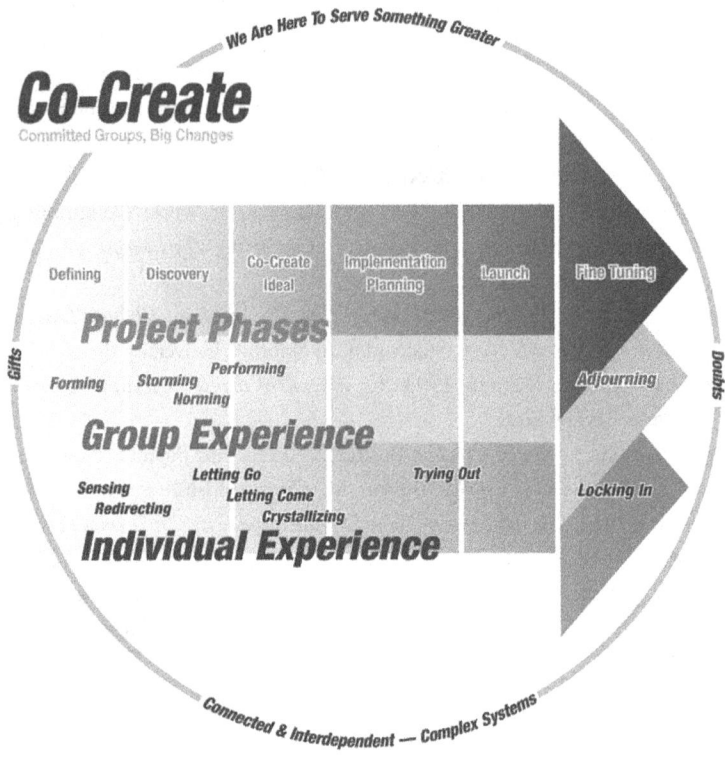

Index

Sharmer, Otto, 7
short-term wins, change process, 81
Smith, Douglas K., 67–68
SOS department and special order
      agents, 107–110
sourcing agents, 98
sponsor, 8
storming
  and norming, 33–34
  team development, 6
  Tuckman model, 83

team commitment. *See also*
      commitment
  creating, 67–68
team development, 89
team facilitator, 9, 60–61
Team Handbook, The, 82
team members, 9
32-Foot Process Map, 35–36
transactional position (TBD), 90–91

trying out (prototyping)
  change process, 78
  U model, 7
Tuckman, Bruce, 83
Tuckman model, team development,
    5–7
Turner, Suzanne, 71, 72

U model, 7–8
uncertainty, 72–73
unfreezing, change process, 76
urgency, change process, 80

vision for change, change process,
    81
visual analysis, 63–64
vulnerability-based trust, 69

whitepaper, 27, 85–89. *See also*
    nonstock white paper
Wisdom of Teams, The, 67–68

OTHER TITLES IN OUR PORTFOLIO AND
PROJECT MANAGEMENT COLLECTION

Timothy J. Kloppenborg, Editor

- *Making Projects Sing: A Musical Perspective of Project Management* by Raji Sivaraman and Chris Wilson
- *Project Teams: A Structured Development Approach* by Vittal S. Anantatmula
- *Attributes of Project-Friendly Enterprises* by Vittal S. Anantatmula and Parviz F. Rad
- *Stakeholder-led Project Management: Changing the Way We Manage Projects* by Louise Worsley
- *KNOWledge SUCCESSion: Sustained Performance and Capability Growth Through Strategic Knowledge Projects* by Arthur Shelley
- *Improving Executive Sponsorship of Projects: A Holistic Approach* by Dawne Chandler and Payson Hall
- *Innovative Business Projects: Breaking Complexities, Building Performance, Volume I; Fundamentals and Project Environment* by Rajagopal
- *Innovative Business Projects: Breaking Complexities, Building Performance, Volume II; Financials, New Insights, and Project Sustainability* by Rajagopal

Announcing the Business Expert Press Digital Library

Concise e-books business students need for classroom and research

This book can also be purchased in an e-book collection by your library as

- a one-time purchase,
- that is owned forever,
- allows for simultaneous readers,
- has no restrictions on printing, and
- can be downloaded as PDFs from within the library community.

Our digital library collections are a great solution to beat the rising cost of textbooks. E-books can be loaded into their course management systems or onto students' e-book readers.
The **Business Expert Press** digital libraries are very affordable, with no obligation to buy in future years. For more information, please visit **www.businessexpertpress.com/librarians**. To set up a trial in the United States, please email **sales@businessexpertpress.com**.

www.ingramcontent.com/pod-product-compliance
Lightning Source LLC
Chambersburg PA
CBHW072313210326
41519CB00057B/4904